HACKING THE WRITING WORKSHOP

HACKING THE WRITING WORKSHOP

Redesign with Making in Mind

Angela Stockman

PUBLICATIONS

Published by Times 10
Highland Heights, OH
HackLearning.org

Project Management by Kelly Schuknecht
Cover Design by Tracey Henterly
Interior Design by Steven Plummer
Editing by Jennifer Jas
Proofreading by Carrie White-Parrish

Library of Congress Cataloging-in-Publication Data is available.
ISBN: 978-1-948212-00-7
First Printing: March, 2018

CONTENTS

DEDICATION

IF YOU WERE once a student of mine and I asked you to sit down and quiet down in order to get print down, this one's for you. I'm sorry, and thank you. You've made me a better teacher.

INTRODUCTION
The perils of print paralysis

THANKS TO THE immediacy of the web, writers of all ages and experience levels have access to audiences that print-only spaces have previously denied them. Digital publishing dominates the industry, and today's writers need an entirely different skill set in order to be influential there. This creates new opportunities and challenges for writing workshop teachers and the learners they support.

The web is shifting the balance of power by democratizing the tools of creation, production, marketing, and distribution. Now, anyone with internet access can turn an idea into a desirable product or a much-needed solution. Then with the push of a button, one can launch it into the world, where it will land inside of a wide market. This is completely transforming industry, as hobbyists are becoming professionals and even entrepreneurs. It's changing how we publish as well.

Today's writers can say anything they want to anyone they want anytime they want, and they can share their work on a scale that we've never experienced before. But in a world where anyone can be immediately published, they must produce work that stands out, is influential, and is worth sharing. Those who have important contributions to make no longer need approval to do so, but they do need a skill set that's often missing from traditional writing workshops. They must master far more than print, process, or craft. They must be multi-medium designers who integrate diverse forms in order to communicate, engage, and serve.

Now the balance of power is squarely with the writers who are design thinkers: those who practice empathy and creative problem-solving in order to make things that matter to others using diverse tools. This might be great news for those who believe they can't write, but it can be discomforting for those who assume that they can, simply because they've mastered print. If we're to support our students well, we need to get clear about what writing really is and isn't in this not-so-new world. We also need to work toward far more relevant interpretations of writing quality. In my experience, the permanency of print often paralyzes talented writers who just happen to struggle with words. It breeds false confidence in self-assured wordsmiths as well.

The beauty of design thinking is that it celebrates so many of the values that teachers have always tried to cultivate in their classrooms: compassion, self-directed learning, thoughtful communication, invention, experimentation, creativity, and teamwork. This, in and of itself, might be enough to inspire you to leverage its connection to writing. There's more, though: design thinkers of all ages and all walks of life engage wider and far more diverse audiences. Making, after all, is a universal language.

Chris Anderson, former editor-in-chief of *Wired* magazine, suggests that over the past decade, we've experienced a significant shift in the amount of time we spend reading content crafted by amateurs for the web, instead of reading professionally created work. This reality has significant implications for those who teach and write inside of our workshops and studios. It also illuminates the significance of design. Our purposes, outlets, and genres are constantly evolving. The most creative expression is multisensory, multimodal expression, and this changes everything about what it means to write well.

Future-ready writers are courageous explorers who know how to sit with discomfort. They're other-centered and attuned to inequity and privilege. They're committed to learning more about those who are different from them and experiences they've never had, to create things that change the way people think and feel and live. They consider the consequences of only writing about what they know. They consider whose voices are missing, whose stories need to be told, and who is disenfranchised. They write for the world, not for themselves or the small audiences they find inside of their classrooms, homes, and local communities.

Future-ready writers also consider the consequences of replicating form. They must iterate on the familiar while inventing things that are entirely new in order to delight, empower, or call their readers to action.

How might we begin to change the way our students define writing? How might we encourage more students to define themselves as writers? Our answers to these questions may increase the likelihood that our students will influence the world in real ways.

Today's readers consume multimodal material through diverse mediums. This realization inspired me to make small but steady changes as a writing teacher and a coach to other teachers who design and facilitate writing workshops. I came to realize that design thinking gave all of us new eyes, ears, and words for these concepts that are already ingrained in young writers. Our thinking about the process had been rooted solidly in the past, and it began to grow into a more current reality.

If you read my first book, *Make Writing: 5 Teaching Strategies that Turn Writer's Workshop into a Maker Space,* then you know that my work began with the study of resistant writers. Those early experiences taught me something important: The kids who were confident with print sometimes struggled to express themselves using other modalities and mediums, and the kids who were confident with maker forms of expression sometimes struggled with print.

Coaching kids to share their diverse expertise inspired everyone to begin practicing courage and humility all at once. Kids knew that they had important strengths and that their perspectives and skills were valued. They also realized that others understood and knew how to do things that they did not. Soon, writers began turning to one another for support. Regardless of their comfort level with print or other tools, everyone in our community began defining themselves as writers, and everyone contributed. More important—everyone wanted to.

This book deepens the conversation that I began in *Make Writing* by challenging teachers to redefine what writing is and how we might help students create it inside of future-ready workshops. Here, kids with wildly diverse strengths make writing that is of real influence in the world. Here, our students become our greatest teachers, collaborators, and leaders. They learn how to assess the constantly shifting interests and needs of their audiences. The curriculum they consume and the work they create flexes in response to their discoveries. And so does the way we teach, assess, and intervene. This book provides the tools you need to put theory into practice.

We'll begin by studying how design thinking elevates the writing process and enriches the workshop experience. I'll challenge our traditional definition of writing, distinguishing *form* from *medium* and *modality*. Then, I'll share my observations about four specific ways that making and writing connect inside of my workshops and studios. We'll explore inexpensive yet powerful ways to renovate your space, and how compassionate practices help cultivate interdependence. I will provide simple curriculum frameworks and we'll explore various ways to situate workshop among other portions of your literacy block and your required programs. I'll also share strategies for supporting student-generated curriculum.

Once you've framed your year and the units that live inside of it, I'll help you make room for loose parts play. You'll learn how to help writers block their drafts and tinker through the writing process, elevating quality bit by bit while building confidence and stamina. Finally, we'll unpack an elegant protocol that will enable you to document learning on your feet and throughout the process, as opposed to merely evaluating final drafts. We'll explore other promising protocols for framing better feedback, and I'll share ideas on how to coach writers to ask for and provide it.

Throughout this text, I'll reference two kinds of making and writing: low-res prototypes and perfected works (see Image I.1). Prototypes are generated by writers largely for themselves and other writers. In the future-ready workshop, we use them to generate ideas, clarify thinking, or explore perspectives. We build low-res prototypes quickly using cheap materials, and we take them down once they've served their purpose to move us and our work forward. Perfected works are created by makers for authentic audiences and consumers. These are high-quality products that creatives perfect for people who will truly appreciate them. They require time, specialized resources, and skills. Perfected works enable writers to bring their messages to the world without relying on print. Both kinds of builds are essential inside the future-ready writing workshop, and I will show you how to teach them through each of the ten Hacks in this book.

Prototypes vs. Perfected Works

Prototypes	Perfected Works
A prototype is created quickly and inexpensively, in order to clarify thinking, explore diverse perspectives, test ideas and solutions, and experiment with point of view.	A perfected work requires time, talent, and specialized materials and resources. Prototyping supports the development of these products, but not all prototypes result in perfected works.
Prototypes are made by makers and writers for makers and writers, in order to move their learning and work forward.	Perfected works are created by makers and writers for authentic audiences who will genuinely appreciate and use them.

Image I.1: Distinguishing low-res prototyping
from the production of perfected works

I've designed this book to allow for differentiated reading experiences. You may carve your own learning pathway as you move from one topic to the next, and the depth of your path will depend on your choices. The text itself illuminates the surface of each hack, but at the end of each one you will find a QR code that links to a supplemental resources folder with additional materials, design thinking tools, and challenges that will help you transform learning into action. Simply download a QR code reader app (such as i-nigma) on your mobile device so you can scan each code. Spend time exploring these resources, and as you dive into your studies, feel free to connect with me on Twitter @AngelaStockman. You'll also find me in the Building Better Writers Facebook group. These are new and experimental practices, and I look forward to exploring them with you.

HACK 1

DESIGN A FUTURE-READY WORKSHOP

Teaching writing in an ever-changing world

Orthodoxies continually make us use old data,
without today's fresh evidence. Orthodoxies make
us tell old stories about children at the expense of
the new stories children are telling us today.
— DONALD GRAVES, WRITING PROCESS VISIONARY AND WORKSHOP PIONEER

THE PROBLEM: LIFT-AND-DROP WRITING
WORKSHOPS ARE BASED ON THE PAST

I REMEMBER MY FIRST introduction to writing workshop. I was a junior in college, completing my final seminar before student teaching, and the professor who I admired most throughout my undergraduate career assigned the book *In the Middle: Writing, Reading, and Learning with Adolescents* by Nancie Atwell. He told us that our class would function as a writing workshop that semester. The experience was transformational. That semester, I became a writer because my professor positioned himself as a learner who sat beside me, spoke with me at length about my work, and helped me realize that my words were worthy of a wider audience. He encouraged me to publish, he connected me to other professors who guided my path, and he ensured that I became a teacher who wrote with my students.

After that experience, I remember preparing my first classroom, greeting my students, and launching my first writing workshop. I channeled both my professor and the great author Nancie Atwell, plus every ounce of my energy I could muster. But despite all that, my new curriculum and my practice failed rather spectacularly.

Soon after, vendors started packaging simple writing workshop units that I could purchase and follow line by carefully scripted line, and at first, I was delighted. These lift-and-drop workshops served me well for some time (they are fine for beginners), but there are two problems with these prefabricated units: their over-reliance on what the past has taught us about writing and young writers, and the way they typically position teachers at the front of the entire process.

Today, Pinterest is full of writing workshop units, and when teachers ask me if these units are worth their time and money, I suggest that they proceed with caution. While lift-and-drop workshops expose us to tried-and-true structures and help us adopt important research-based practices, they're not enough anymore. If we want to create future-ready writers who sustain real influence inside a fast-paced and unpredictable world, we must learn how to treat teaching as a learning process and how to make our students our greatest mentors. Traditional writing workshops position teachers as experts who guide the study of common forms. Future-ready writers mix, remix, and create their own, and they invite their teachers and peers to learn beside them. This typically requires far more than words. In my experience, it inspires the use of different mediums, modalities, and processes that look like making.

THE HACK: DESIGN A FUTURE-READY WORKSHOP

Design thinking is a very human endeavor. It helps writing teachers make decisions about curriculum, instruction, assessment, and process based on evidence from their current and rapidly changing realities. Rather than relying on outdated scores or our own biased instincts, teaching writing by design empowers us to develop timely insights about the strengths and needs of the writers we support, and to provide far more relevant responses. Design thinking makes us agile teachers, and agile teachers produce agile writers who can sustain their influence in the world.

So, how might you begin to explore the relationship between design thinking and the writing process? Visuals like Image 1.1 can be clarifying, but a few words of caution: They can also be misleading.

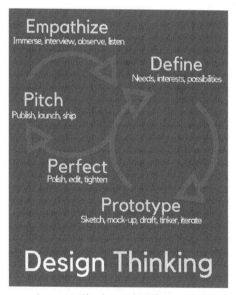

Image 1.1: The design thinking process

Design thinking isn't a linear process, and it isn't sequential; there are many ways to work each phase to its fullest potential. This image is a simple illustration of a process that can be delightfully complex and include vast opportunities for creative application. If you're interested in exploring the complexities of design thinking, you'll find a set of my favorite design thinking tools in the supplemental resources folder at the end of this Hack.

I also learn a great deal from my colleagues in the #MakeWriting, #dtk12chat, and #designthinking communities on Twitter. Drop by and say hello.

In my world, design thinking involves five distinct phases:

1. Assessing interests and needs to deepen our empathy for those we intend to serve,

2. Generating and considering a variety of creative approaches for satisfying those interests and needs,

3. Tinkering with the most promising options to assess their fit and effectiveness,

4. Committing to the approach that demonstrates the best results, perfecting our work, and finally,

5. Pitching our products.

> WHEN YOU SHARE YOUR THINKING, LEARNING, AND WORK WITH THOSE WHO ARE DIFFERENT FROM YOU, IT DEEPENS YOUR PRACTICE, PUSHES YOUR THINKING, AND PREVENTS YOU FROM CREATING AND TEACHING INSIDE OF YOUR OWN ECHO CHAMBER.

Consider how this process compares to others you've used in your work. In my experience, most teachers practice some of the elements of design intuitively, in much the same way beginners teach themselves distinct guitar chords without much thought or intention. How might you begin to choreograph the whole of your practice? How might you blend these single chords into a beautiful piece of music?

The ideas that follow will give you a quick start (is tomorrow quick enough?), and the Blueprint for Full Implementation section will help you carry your work forward.

WHAT YOU CAN DO TOMORROW

Start by practicing empathy. Survey your students about their interests in writing and other creative expression. Help them define their strengths and uncover their needs. As much as possible, start to immerse yourself in their worlds: Spend time in their communities and get acquainted with the issues that matter most to them. Eventually, use what you discover to transform your curriculum and your practices, and solicit their feedback on the changes along the way. Here are five quick ways to gather real-time, relevant data that can help you create and sustain a future-ready writing workshop.

- **HELP WRITERS DEFINE THEIR INTERESTS AND NEEDS.** What would you rather be doing if you didn't have to write right now? What do you like to make? What do you like to read? What are your favorite television programs? Which movies do you like best? What activities do you enjoy participating in outside of school? What are your favorite subjects? What do you want to get better at as a writer? How do you want to grow as a learner?

How can I help you? How can you help us? Invite writers to thoughtfully reflect on questions like these before sharing their responses with you or the group. You'll find creative ways to do so in the supplemental resources folder for this Hack.

- **INVITE STUDENTS TO SHARE THEIR EXPERTISE.** Define what you feel you "must do" in order to teach the requisite content and skills for this unit. Many teachers will define at least one element of craft that they want to help writers perfect. Craft includes ideas, organization, word choice, sentence fluency, and voice. Writing teachers are also eager to teach skills that support each phase of the writing process including brainstorming, drafting, revision, and editing skills. Finally, teachers ensure the quality of the work produced by teaching specific lessons about the form of the piece itself. What must be taught about narrative, argument, or information writing? Are you supporting a different form or a multi-genre piece? What do you feel responsible for helping your students learn? Define these "must do's" clearly for your students. Then, invite them to share their expertise about any of these concepts or skills. Create a living document or display that allows writers to name, share, and tap into each other's strengths rather than relying exclusively on you for guidance and support.

- **GATHER NEW MODELS AND MENTOR TEXTS.** In traditional writing workshops, teachers use mentor texts—the works of other authors—to model specific craft moves. Writing by design challenges writers to curate a wide collection of multi-modal mentor texts, including the integration of diverse mediums. The examples writers collect align with their personal interests and the kinds of work they're most interested in making themselves. You'll find my favorites in the supplemental resources folder for this Hack. Encourage your students to create a collection of their own favorites. How might you use their collections to inform what you teach, how you teach it, and the kinds of work you inspire your students to create?

- **SOLICIT TARGETED FEEDBACK FROM YOUR STUDENTS.** It's very helpful to ask the writers I support how I might make our next session even more worthwhile for them. How can I best help you? What do I need to change? What do you need to do more often? What should I do less? What helps? What hurts? How can I do this better? These are the questions I share at the end of every class, and I often collect student responses on an exit ticket before they head out the door, or digitally, using apps like Kahoot! or with Google Forms or Mentimeter.

- **COACH WRITERS TO PRACTICE EMPATHY, TOO.** Great writers know their readers well enough to satisfy their interests and needs. Invite your students to define topics for their writing that interest them, but then, teach them to consider which of those topics might be meaningful and relevant to others as well. One of the easiest ways to do this is to invite writers to post a list of potential topics in a space where classmates might provide feedback on them. Rather than diving into a project that centers solely around a topic of their own choosing, they might invite their classmates, friends, and even family members to share the topics that are of most interest to them. You'll find an empathy-building game that can be played in a single class period in the supplemental resources folder for this hack as well.

A BLUEPRINT FOR FULL IMPLEMENTATION

Step 1: Become a globally connected learner.

While integrating empathetic practices is a great first step toward teaching writing by design, it's important to connect and learn from others who are also using these methods to support learners of all kinds. It's also valuable to gain perspective about how design thinking is used in other industries and fields—because what's happening in your writing workshop is preparing many students for that world.

It's all too easy to schoolify design, and reduce it to an efficient and formulaic practice, but this will render it ineffective. When you share your thinking, learning, and work with those who are different from you, it deepens your practice, pushes your thinking, and prevents you from creating and teaching inside of your own echo chamber.

Consider joining Twitter if you haven't already, and connect to the #dtk12chat, #designthinking, and #makewriting communities there. You are welcome to follow me @AngelaStockman, and I'll be happy to introduce you to those who have helped me along the way.

Step 2: Treat programs as prototypes.

On the market today are several incredibly well-designed programs that guide the implementation of writing workshops. I tend to remain program-agnostic, as each is only as good as the system it's living in, but in general I'm a fan of any tool that provides pathways and support for uncertain teachers. Often, programs aren't the problem inside of our schools. The problem is how we as teachers tend to use them.

A new program is like any other prototype: It's a preliminary model in need of thorough and careful testing. This isn't how we always treat new programs, though. Instead, we invest a fortune in full-scale purchases, and then we demand sustained fidelity to the scripts embedded in them. Please don't misunderstand me; fidelity is an important part of testing a program well, but so is gathering data about the program's effect on learners and teachers and classrooms and school cultures and any number of other factors that matter very much to us. Over time, I've learned that there are those who purchase programs because they're seeking options and are eager to experiment with new ideas, and there are those who purchase programs to teacher-proof their schools. The first intention has merit. The latter threatens professional development and practice, over time.

The following questions will help guide your thinking when it comes to new programs. How could you take a design approach as you implement the programs your school has adopted? How might you use what you've learned from your empathy work to make promising adaptations to the program? How can you gather evidence of the effect of these adjustments on your writers? What is your vision for a future-ready workshop? How will you know if your program is helping you achieve it? What can you study? More importantly, how will you use your findings?

Step 3: Study the relationship between the writing process and design thinking.

I've taken some time to sketch what I've noticed about the relationship between the writing process and design thinking so far (see Image 1.2). Rather than framing them as a series of steps, I prefer to think of them as phases of creative work or even stances we might assume. My thinking is still evolving here, but it's solid enough to share.

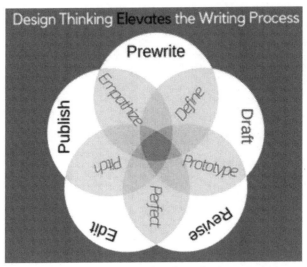

Image 1.2: Exploring the relationship between
the writing process and design thinking

Like design thinking, the writing process isn't linear, and it isn't as simple or efficient as most visual models suggest. Both support iteration: repeating processes while making small adjustments to get better results. Feedback drives good design thinking, and it also empowers the writing process. It elevates the quality of the work by grounding writers in empathy and allowing potential readers to have a voice in the creationary process from the outset. This increases the writer's likelihood of becoming truly influential.

Rather than teaching students to simply brainstorm, design thinking helps them get to know their intended audiences and write especially for them. Rather than merely executing on a single idea that entices the writer alone, design thinking invites creatives to tinker with different approaches to notice what might wow their intended audiences. And rather than settling for print, design thinking encourages writers to translate their works through different mediums and modalities, creating multisensory experiences that others will find meaningful and memorable. Design thinking requires writers to consider much more than their words. It motivates them to write for worthy purposes, to tuck well-crafted print inside of beautiful, handmade packages, and to deliver it all efficiently and effectively to the people they hope to influence.

If you were to draw the relationship between the writing process and design, what would your visual look like?

Step 4: Let writers choose additional mediums and modalities for their finished works.

When we distinguish form from medium and modality, we lower the barriers that paralyze print-resistant kids, and we help print-proficient writers expand their narrow skill sets. Each unit in a writing workshop challenges writers to produce specific forms. This is a traditional practice that has great value, as it enables teachers to coach the standards of craft.

Figure 1.3 illustrates the distinction between forms, modalities, mediums, and outlets. I find that sharing these possibilities with print-resistant writers provides new entry points for their learning and work. Perhaps they won't begin with print, and that's okay. This table also challenges those who assume that print proficiency makes them great writers. This is a necessary discomfort.

Examples of Forms, Modalities, Mediums, and Outlets

Forms:	Examples of Genre: Narrative, Opinion, Persuasion, Argument, Informative
	Examples of Mode: Small Moment Story, Editorial, Public Service Announcement, Explainer Video
Modalities:	Naturalist, Intrapersonal, Interpersonal, Bodily/Kinesthetic, Spatial/Visual, Musical, Logical, Linguistic
Mediums:	Paint, Wood, Metal, Stone, Clay, Pottery, Acrylic, Chalk, Charcoal, Ink, Pencil, Pastel, Crayon, Marker, LEGO, Graphic Art Software, Animation Software, Design Apps, Digital Printing, Stop Motion, Programming, Coding, Chef's Tools, Letterpress, Website Development, Paper, Our Bodies, Screen Printing, Instruments, Collage, Game Design, Fabric
Outlets:	Websites, Blogs, Instagram, Facebook, Twitter, SnapChat, Letters to Editors, Letters to School, Community, State, Federal Leaders, Contests, Online Writing Communities, Industry Journals, Magazines, Self-Published Books, Google Classroom, Publishing Apps, Showcasing or Selling at Craft or County Fairs, Maker Faires, Education Conferences, Podcasts, Live Video, Gifting Others with Words and Handmade Items, Guest Teaching, Guest Posting, Digital Portfolios, EdCamps

Figure 1.3: Distinguishing forms from mediums, modalities, and outlets

Many of the world's most influential makers choose mediums and modalities other than print to tell stories, make arguments, and teach audiences about the world around them. They know that when their creations trigger multiple senses all at once, their audiences are transported to new and unexpected places. They know that the mediums they choose are just as important as their messages, and that writing is about far more than words. This is why prioritizing print prevents many young writers from becoming influential in the world. Truly powerful writers consider how different approaches play across varied outlets, and by doing so they expand their audiences.

In addition to producing written drafts, invite writers to

experiment and even perfect their use of other mediums or modalities. Help them launch these perfected works into the world using skillfully selected outlets. You do not need to master these tools yourself. You simply need to assess how well your students are able to identify, test, and evaluate the appropriateness of the outlets they choose. Ideal outlets are those that best connect writers with their intended audiences. Successful writers consistently assess their influence. Many outlets include tools that show metrics. This is an important skill that future-ready writers rely on. In the supplemental resources folder, you'll find a guidance document that will help you and your students to make thoughtful choices about forms, mediums, modalities, and outlets.

Step 5: Share feedback on what matters most, when it matters most.

As teachers of writing, we are called to help our students grow and improve in the process and quality of their work. Our curricula are aligned to specific standards of quality—our own and those our region, state, or country define for us. And our effectiveness is often measured, formally and informally, by our ability to help writers meet these standards. To accomplish this, I find it far more effective to assess a writer's progress frequently throughout the process rather than evaluating completed drafts. When I assess portions of student writing bit by bit, my feedback is timely, targeted, and offered in a dose that writers can immediately respond to. I'm better able to intervene when my assessments are frequent and focused. This is another benefit of practicing design thinking: It reduces the risks inherent in valuing products over processes. This practice elevates the quality of the drafts that students submit, and it helps me foster good relationships with kids, too.

As writers translate print into other mediums and modalities, my purposes and my stance shift a bit. I encourage writers to take big risks, trying methods and using materials that we may be completely unfamiliar with. Often, I don't have the capacity to teach kids how to use these resources, as they are almost limitless and always growing and changing. More important, I don't want to teach students how to use them. I want them to fiddle, tinker, and play. I want them to collaborate and build a sort of collective intelligence that the entire community might benefit from. I want them to know stuff that I don't know, and I want them to turn to one another for help rather than relying on me. I want their work to be experimental and innovative, too. This means they're going to fail at times, and it means that they may not finish. And that's okay, because when it comes to creating perfected works, learning matters more than finishing.

Rather than meeting a specific set of standards that align to quality, I want students to look for evidence of conventionality in the work of masterful creatives who they've identified as their mentors. When a writer hopes to translate his argument into a meme, I ask him to locate examples of memes he'd like to emulate or iterate on. When another expresses an interest in creating a public service announcement, I invite her to find great examples first. Then, once multiple models have been located, I ask that writers unpack them and ask themselves: What do I notice about most of the work created with this medium or in this modality? Why might these trends exist? What does this suggest about conventionality? How will I try this in my own work? How will I show that my awareness of conventionality is informing what I do? You'll notice how I help writers attend to these issues in the project proposal guidance document, located in the supplemental resources folder.

Step 6: Triangulate your data.

When we triangulate our data, we look for trends and anomalies in at least three different data sources captured using different research methods. For example, I might study standardized test results, local performance-based assessment results, and annotated records captured during learning conferences with kids to better understand a writer's strengths and needs.

How would my perspective change if I only looked at the annotated records? What if I only examined standardized test results? Triangulation is a best practice for teachers who are using data in any context or capacity, but I find it particularly vital when I'm practicing design. Empathy requires that we come to know our students. It requires our students to come to know their audiences as well. This means that we must be conscious of the role that self-awareness plays in anyone's ability to name and share their interests and needs.

Teachers have the power to help their students deepen their self-awareness, making what was once unconscious, conscious. The same can be said for writers. Triangulation inspires us to ask ourselves which important stories haven't been told, so that we might get that data on the table. When we do, it often reveals new perspectives that inform our processes. If you're interested in learning more about how to gather, analyze, and craft meaningful stories about the data you collect, visit the supplemental resources folder for this Hack.

OVERCOMING PUSHBACK

Designing a future-ready writing workshop means grappling with uncertainty. When we practice empathy and coach writers to do the same, we put the needs and interests of others ahead of our own, and relinquish an awful lot of control. This demands a shift in our priorities and a willingness to treat teaching as the experiment it is rather than maintaining false certainty about what will or will not work. Pushback is common, and in fact, it's welcome. These are some of the thoughts that my favorite skeptics shared with me as I began recommending teaching by design. Perhaps you'll recognize yourself or another colleague in my examples.

We don't have time to translate print into other mediums or modalities. What if you compacted your writing workshop curriculum to make time for this important work? If you think about it, the kinds of experiences that create lifelong writers who influence the world are not just those that result in the completion of tasks and forms—it is the experiences that connect writers to real audiences who appreciate the complexity and originality of their work. If your end goal is to create excellent future-ready writers, you can find the time to update your writing workshop.

I'm required to use a specific program with complete fidelity. Perhaps you could design an action research project and use a sample group to study the effect of these practices on engagement, evidence of learning, creativity, improved quality, or growth. Expectations about fidelity typically begin to shift when school leaders gain evidence-based perspectives about alternative approaches and interventions that work.

My most print-proficient writers resist the use of diverse modalities and mediums. Remember, it's important to distinguish low-res prototypes from perfected, finished products. When makers prototype, they use inexpensive materials to rapidly produce simple models that enable them to think differently and express themselves without print. This is low-risk, low-cost, and rapid-pace making, and it's very different from creating perfected, multi-modal or mixed media products for audiences who will consume them. This kind of building moves the writer forward. The stakes are lower, and so is the time commitment. While many print-resistant kids commit to creating beautiful works of art for audiences that will appreciate them, this simpler prototype making is intended to serve the writer alone, and might appeal more to your print-proficient students. I talk more about this in Hack 8.

My school leaders value standardized assessment data more than any other kind. Sometimes it's difficult to help others appreciate the data that emerges in other contexts. While standardized assessment data might make the surface of students' strengths and needs visible, the data we collect on our feet, during instruction, often provides critical insights that help to explain test performance. You may use the qualitative data that you gather in far more complex and meaningful ways, as well. If you feel that your school leaders aren't appreciative of its power, sharing your learning and work with them might inspire change.

THE HACK IN ACTION

High school teacher Dan Ryder, co-author of *Intention: Critical Creativity in the Classroom* and the Education Director of the Success and Innovation Center at Mt. Blue Campus in Farmington, Maine, created a student-centered area inside of his high school that fuses design, socio-emotional support and development, academic advising, and maker education into one space. Here, students pursue passions and possibilities by practicing self-awareness and empathy.

Inspired by Ivan Kroghurd, co-founder, former CEO, and lead strategist at a software company called QuestBack, Dan immersed his students in a design thinking challenge wherein all learners researched and then created user manuals ... *for themselves*. In an interview with the *New York Times*, Ivan explained that often, the teams that he was a part of suffered unnecessary anxiety and lost productive work time grappling with the tensions that arose when teammates failed to understand how to work with one another.

The user manual helps people adapt to different values, behaviors, and beliefs by encouraging everyone to make their personal preferences transparent. Rather than wasting time trying to figure one another out and mediating frequent misunderstandings, user manuals enable group members to name their values, pet peeves, what they have patience for, what makes them lose it, and how people can help and understand them better. Dan thought it would be important for his students to experiment with this practice because it seemed more active and engaging than the traditional interest survey. This process provided his students immediate immersion into the design thinking mindset.

The students in Dan's design lab, a mix of new and experienced design thinkers, explored multiple models as they produced their rough drafts, and they asked their friends to provide feedback. This offered quite a bit of perspective. Students discovered that while they might have provided a great deal of information about themselves, many chose delivery methods that appealed to either their strengths or their desire to find a path of least resistance. Those that were most successful considered their users, and created engaging, interactive, informative, and resonant manuals.

If you're interested in reviewing this process in its entirety, scan Image 1.4 below to drop into the supplemental resources folder. There you'll find links to Dan's work.

Pam Taylor, a kindergarten and first-grade makerspace facilitator from Aylesbury Public School in Ontario, Canada, began her new year by challenging young writers to use a variety of loose parts to tell their classmates about something that they were good at. Her intention was to help writers recognize and name their strengths, in order to recognize the contributions they might make to their writing community. She wanted every writer in the room to see the teacher in every one, rather than positioning herself at the center of her workshop. This was a tall order for such young writers, and she knew that building might help her students find success.

"Our students are familiar with using loose parts and creating pictures with them," Pam told me. "I wanted them to communicate their ideas and information orally, in a clear and coherent manner because this is what our standards expect. I also wanted them to be able to see and include important details."

These are skills that print writing demands, and Pam was confident that even her youngest and least experienced writers would be able to use them well. She could have invited her students to draw or to simply speak, as these are common scaffolds for primary writers who are not yet comfortable with print. Pam was eager to engage them and invite diverse perspectives about their personal strengths, though. She knew that building would inspire far more creativity and help them see themselves and one another differently. Materials matter. She knew she needed a mix.

Using loose parts enabled Pam's students to name their strengths in a detailed manner. This resulted in wildly varied representations that enhanced their oral communication efforts. "Many of my students are English language learners," Pam revealed. "Building helps them express themselves more fully. They can make the ideas that they do not yet have words for. Others struggle with small motor skills, which makes printing difficult. Building their responses gives them confidence."

Building helped Pam assess, reflect, and set meaningful instructional goals, too. "I'm going to challenge them to start labeling their builds," she told me. "Many of my students have a grasp of initial sounds and the beginnings of words. I'll encourage them to try labeling their representations next. We're building empathy for one another every day by sharing our work with friends, discussing what we're good at, turning to one another and not just the teacher for support, and setting goals."

Pam's students have taught her a great deal, and her willingness to learn from them is improving her planning and instruction as she prepares them for the future.

When teachers position themselves as design thinkers and coach their students to do the same, the learning that emerges is directly aligned to real-time experiences and the authentic needs and interests of the audiences they serve. Practicing empathy and prototyping our plans stands in stark contrast to teaching and writing that is driven by traditional orthodoxies and prefabricated programs. Encouraging writers to translate print through diverse mediums and modalities increases the value of their work and the likelihood that they will be of real influence in the world.

None of this looks like the writing workshop my beloved college professor introduced me to, but I'm certain he'd be okay with the shifts I'm recommending. In my experience, elevating design and encouraging making inside of a future-ready workshop has another important effect as well: It enhances the quality of the writing that students produce there. Hack 2 will introduce you to the four ways I notice this happening.

Before you go, be sure to scan the QR code below to check out all of those additional resources I promised you. Here are a few things you'll find inside:

- Design thinking tools and routines

- Creative approaches for assessing the needs and interests of your students

- Examples of student expertise on display

- Multi-modal mentor texts and those created with varied mediums

- A guidance document that will help writers make thoughtful choices about form, medium, and modality

- An additional guidance document that will help you gather and analyze meaningful data to tell your learning stories

Image 1.4: Scan the code to find supplemental resources for supporting Hack 1.

HACK 2

RECOGNIZE AND ENGAGE THE MAKER IN YOUR MIDST

Four ways building breeds better writers

Your hands are the original digital devices. Use them.

AUSTIN KLEON, WRITER AND ARTIST

THE PROBLEM: STUDENTS WHO STRUGGLE WITH WRITING

IF YOU READ *Make Writing: 5 Teaching Strategies That Turn Writer's Workshop Into a Maker Space*, then you know that I came to these discoveries honestly and painfully, on my hands and knees and waving a big white flag. The fact was that I surrendered, and it was only then that I entertained the notion of making inside of my workshop. It wasn't even my idea. I simply gave in. I caved.

You might remember six-year-old Luke and the tears he shed all over my classroom floor. You might remember how I tried everything to get him to write, but he wasn't having any of it. No how. No way. And so I asked, "What would you rather be doing right now, if you didn't have to write?" He told me he wanted his Legos, and because I had no fight left, I finally let him have his way. It was a turning point in my own learning story.

That summer, Luke taught me and a bunch of other teachers how to write with Legos. In the years that followed, countless other kids connected their making lives to their writing lives in ways I could not predict, nor strive to manage. I created opportunities and gave them permission to make, and they showed up and taught me more than I ever could have imagined.

A bit of clarification, though: What I learned may have been unexpected, but the fact that it happened and the way that it happened was quite intentional. In my experience, making is meaningful when it moves writers forward, not when it inspires them to evade the process entirely.

Print still matters, and so does writing performance. Regardless of how resistant writers might be, at the end of the day, we, as teachers, are responsible for engaging them in the process, and when they don't improve, that's on us.

When I invited Luke to make inside of my writing workshop, it was an act of complete desperation. He was unhappy, and I was failing him—hard. It was clear that he was not going to write, and so inviting him to make compromised nothing. In the end, much was gained, including the realization that many students who present as resistant writers are really makers at heart. This was my first, and perhaps, my most profound discovery: Making is a powerful gateway to writing, especially for those who struggle.

THE HACK: RECOGNIZE AND ENGAGE
THE MAKER IN YOUR MIDST

My discovery about making continues to resonate with me, but in recent years, I've learned that making isn't merely an intervention for kids who dislike writing. It's a powerful means for elevating every writer's process and work. In fact, when we make with intention inside of my writing workshops and studios and the classrooms where I coach, we notice improvements in performance.

Making motivates writers, especially when their writing is built around their making. Teachers may choose the form in much the same way we always have in a writer's workshop, but inviting writers to choose their own topics, and more important, to center their drafts around the things they're making, is pretty powerful stuff.

Making also ignites critical thinking and the analysis of form. Amy Burvall and Dan Ryder, the authors of *Intention: Critical Creativity in the Classroom,* inspired me in this area. Given a set of creative constraints (a provocative prompt, a specific set of materials, and limited time, to name a few), how might students rapidly prototype stories, their opinions, or pieces that inform, or even teach? When we invite kids to make their responses, their experiences are richer, and according to Amy and Dan, "stickier" too. Kids remember what they build. I find that quick challenges like these help print-resistant kids make powerful contributions to our learning and work. If you want to reach out to them, Dan is @ WickedDecent on Twitter, and Amy is @AmyBurvall.

While one might think that the finer elements of a subject lend themselves to print, making requires writers to consider things about their topics that they may not have even noticed otherwise. The products that emerge from cycles of making serve as artifacts that invite close analysis. This kind of study helps writers uncover new details that enrich their drafts with nuance and complexity. Making helps writers solve the problems they face when drafting, too.

I often look for signs that a student is a maker—perhaps a blocked writer—and work to especially engage the student in making. I might invite the student to "prototype the part you don't have words for just yet." This invitation is rarely declined, and building almost always moves writers forward.

CREATE THE SPACE AND THE TIME FOR MAKING, LET YOUR STUDENTS KNOW YOU'RE EAGER TO LEARN FROM THEM, AND CHALLENGE THEM TO USE MAKING IN A WAY THAT ELEVATES THEIR WRITING.

Finally, when kids treat print as a collection of loose parts, the resulting work is typically far more inventive. Making writing in this way sustains their stamina, too. Coaching writers to approach any form as a synthesis of blocks makes the modes and genres of writing far more tangible and easier to pull apart and play with. It also enables us to linger over each of them longer. Helping writers draft block by block and bit by bit increases their confidence as they rapidly develop skills, hit their targets with higher frequency, and provide opportunities for feedback and intervention daily or even multiple times a day. I'll share more on this in Hack 8. In the meantime, here are four things you can do tomorrow to leverage making in service to writing.

WHAT YOU CAN DO TOMORROW

These are the most promising practices that I've unearthed by making writing with kids of all ages and all interests and ability levels. I hope you add your own practices, based upon your experiences. Share your ideas in the #MakeWriting stream on Twitter. You may inspire other teachers who follow this topic.

- **INVITE WRITERS TO USE MOMENTS FROM THEIR MAKING LIVES TO FUEL THEIR WRITTEN WORK.**
  Have you ever asked your students what they like to make outside of school or what they're working on in other school-sponsored spaces that they find particularly compelling? In Hack I, we examined different ways to practice empathy at the start of new learning experiences. Consider how you might do this in order to discover your students' making interests. Then, invite them to tap the well of these experiences and define subjects and topics for their writing.

- **OPEN EACH WRITING SESSION WITH A QUICK YET CAREFULLY CRAFTED FIRESTARTER.**
  Firestarters are creative constraints that we bundle together and light at the start of a workshop session. Aligned to that day's teaching point or learning target, firestarters include a provocative prompt, a handful of loose parts for rapid prototyping, and limited time for completion. You'll find an entire slide deck of firestarters waiting for you in the supplemental resources folder at the end of this Hack.

45

- **WHEN WRITERS ARE BLOCKED, PROMPT THEM TO SWITCH MODALITIES OR TRY A DIFFERENT MEDIUM.** When elementary students struggle to reflect a character's emotional evolution in their writing, I invite them to map it out using emojis (see Image 2.1).

Image 2.1: Mapping the emotional evolution of a character with emojis.

When high school writers are eager to design more innovative plot structures, I suggest they tie their story lines onto lengths of string. Then, they play around with the strings. Each bend, knot, and braid generates new and interesting ideas about form. Would you like to see other examples of medium and modality switching? Follow the QR code at the end of this Hack to the supplemental resources folder.

- **TREAT TEXT AND THE ELEMENTS OF FORM LIKE LOOSE PARTS.** Rather than expecting students to write draft after draft, or equipping them with static graphic organizers, why not help them craft each form one small bit at a time? Investigate story hooks, and then tinker with them together. Invite writers to experiment with hooks using three or four different approaches. Expect them to solicit feedback before choosing the one that readers will most likely prefer. Show them how to draft on index cards or sticky notes.

Image 2.2: Ava builds her story bit by bit, treating the text like loose parts.

Let them write on their feet, sprawled across the floor, or on the walls and windows of your classroom. In Hack 8, I will share specific strategies for blocking form and writing bit by bit.

A BLUEPRINT FOR FULL IMPLEMENTATION

Step 1: Do a bit of light action research.

It's easy to lift and drop the four "What You Can Do Tomorrow" approaches above into your own writing workshop, but if you do a bit of action research—even light action research—the rewards may be far greater. Create the space and the time for making, let your students know you're eager to learn from them, and challenge them to use making in a way that elevates their writing. Then, study the results. Document what you see and hear. Gather and analyze student writing samples. Engage kids in baseline and post-assessment writing. And be sure to share what you've learned with your fellow teachers and administrators, and the rest of us in the #MakeWriting stream on Twitter.

Are you uncertain how to begin or what to include in the documentation? Interested in trying baseline and post-assessment work and in need of prompts and tools that can help you make good decisions? Visit the supplemental resources folder at the end of this Hack. There, you'll find guidance documents for documentation, samples of pre- and post-assessments, a protocol that can help you study growth in writing performance, and some of my own action research stories.

Step 2: Break down barriers between your workshop and other classrooms.

I often find myself a bit perplexed when my STEAM-loving friends leave writing out of the making conversation. It's no wonder they're troubled by the notion that writing is exclusive to workshop. I hope each one of us can find ways to collaborate with our colleagues to move writing and making across all content areas. Doing so would buy everyone more time for authentic learning, create greater coherence for students, and enable student-generated learning experiences that integrate inquiry, tinkering, and writing. If you are seriously concerned about improving writing performance, then writing probably needs to happen in every single class every single day. What can you do to bring your teaching team one step closer to that ideal? In the supplemental resources folder for this Hack, you'll find strategies to support writing in multiple content areas. While you're there, peek at some of the action plans to support content area writing systemically as well.

Step 3: Challenge writers to document and reflect upon their making, their writing, and making writing.

Every single thing I've learned about the connection between making and writing emerged from my work with kids. I find that when I slow down and simply watch them and talk with them, they teach me how this works. When I encourage them to document and reflect on their thinking, their learning, their making, and their writing, our discoveries are often profound. We document in many ways. In my writing workshops and studios, writers draw, photograph, video and audio record, and make notes in their writers' notebooks. We stop to reflect on our experiences daily, and I interview and observe them and use a variety of apps to create digital portfolios simply and efficiently. How might you invite your students to document their making and writing experiences? How will you plan to make this a successful endeavor? If you visit the supplemental resources folder for this Hack, you will find abundant materials that will support your beginnings. If you wish to find me on Twitter, we can talk things through there as well.

OVERCOMING PUSHBACK

When teachers begin making writing in their workshops, common challenges arise. These are frequent issues I've watched others face and some of the best ideas I've found for overcoming them.

I don't have time to do action research. It can feel overwhelming, I know. I recommend a simple start and a light approach. Begin by documenting what you see or hear relevant to just one topic. This is how my discoveries about making and writing began. I was eager to help resistant writers. I needed to unlock their potential, so I gave them abundant resources, choices, and a bit of time, and I watched them. Then, when resistant writers started making progress, I documented everything I saw and heard by snapping photos and making recordings with my cell phone. I created albums and eventually, with consent from my students and their parents, I started sharing the class progress on my blog, on Flickr, and in the Building Better Writers Facebook group. I asked my students a whole bunch of questions as time went on, and I leaned in and listened hard when they answered. None of this felt like work because it was something that completely compelled me, and I let it unfold naturally, as the kids and I needed it to.

I suggest starting with the problems you are most interested in solving in your own writing workshop. Start small. Let it be messy. Embrace the uncertainty of it all and good things will emerge.

If I invite one blocked writer to build, the rest of the class will want to stop writing to build, too. I agree—this is often the case when I don't offer consistent opportunities for making to all writers. But when we begin each session with a firestarter, when we begin blocking and tinkering with form bit by bit, and when writers are encouraged to translate print through different mediums and modalities, this problem disappears. If making is a novelty, writers will be distracted by it. If everyone has ample opportunities to build, everyone simply makes writing.

I don't have time to collaborate with colleagues who teach other classes. This is a sad reality for many teachers, and that's why I chose to feature Angie Mullinnex in the Hack in Action below. Angie unwittingly solved the cross-content collaboration issue when she embarked on a Make Writing initiative in her school. She created toolkits for the teachers in her building, and encouraged them to use them in wildly diverse ways. She had just one request: Teachers were expected to share their work by adding it to a binder that traveled with the kit. Face-to-face conversations and gatherings happened as teachers were able to meet, but the binder enabled a sort of asynchronous and efficient collaboration that I'm recommending to others who are faced with this dilemma. How might you create a similar sort of workaround, to foster better collaboration?

THE HACK IN ACTION

When Christine Boyer, an elementary teacher from Heathcote Elementary in Scarsdale, New York, opened her first makerspace, her students taught her that making was a story in itself, and that using the space as a setting could engage writers as well as makers. They came to this realization organically, as they began documenting the learning that was happening in their new space.

"That first year I was taking photos all the time because the makerspace was new," Christine told me. "Not only was I incredibly proud of it, I was fascinated with what was happening in there, how the kids were making it their own—working and teaching one another." Christine positioned herself as an observer while her students set up supplies, asked thoughtful questions, and challenged one another to build and take things apart. "I sat in awe and photographed happily," she said.

Students began voluntarily showing up to make before and after school and during lunch. Their curiosities were compelling conversation starters:

Why is there a magnet in this speaker? Why is this glass curved?

Christine documented their exchanges, and her camera was one of her greatest tools. Soon, she began projecting the images and inviting her students to reflect together. This was a powerful way for each group to see how others were using the space: What they were building, what they were learning, and most important, how.

"Smiles grew every time we gathered for a few quick minutes to look at the photos," Christine said, but there was something more: Narratives began to grow out of these reflections, too.

Christine is a seasoned workshop teacher and has taught narrative writing for some time. "This was different," she explained. "Traditionally we ask kids to recall stories, and then, write them down. This time, the students lived their stories as they wrote them. They evolved slowly and bit by bit as makers reflected on what they were building and learning." Grounding narrative writing in real-time making elevated both experiences for Christine's students. If you want to learn more about how her work has evolved, connect with her on Twitter @5boyer.

Angie Mullinnex, Academic Lead Teacher at Humble Independent School District in Humble, Texas, was so convinced that making would elevate writing in her school that she took it upon herself to launch a collaborative cross-content initiative. Certain that her school would not receive the funding necessary to launch a robust makerspace anytime soon, Angie used large plastic storage tubs to create mobile Make Writing toolkits that moved from one classroom to the next.

Image 2.3: Angie Mullinnex's Make Writing Toolkits

Each toolkit included the following items:

Art roll paper

Register tape

Mini white boards

Dry erase markers

Sticky notes (and a lot of these!)

Markers (colored, washable, and permanent)

Highlighters in various colors

Sidewalk chalk

Blank note cards and envelopes

White T-shirts

White hats

White bandanas

Paint markers

Rory's Story Cubes

Molding clay

Building blocks

Legal pads

Journals

Plastic eggs

Popsicle sticks

Cardstock in various colors

Paper in various colors

Fine-tip black permanent marker (for writing on building blocks)

In addition to these materials, Angie created binders for each kit that provided new users a bit of background and inspiration for making and writing. As kids and teachers tested these kits across different content areas, they designed their own approaches, documented their learning and work, and added photographs, reflections, and ideas to the binders.

Before long, kids were tinkering with the kits in rooms all over the building, and teachers began discovering much about the potential for making to elevate writing in any content area. To chat with Angie about this project, find her on Twitter @DocAngMullinnex.

The tools in the supplemental resources folder below will help you to recognize and engage the makers in your midst, and distinguish form from medium and modality as you consider different approaches for making in the writing workshop. You will find:

- The firestarters slide deck

- Tools that will help you document and study growth in writers and their writing

- Ideas for teaching writing in the content areas

- Examples of medium and modality switching

- A few of my own action research stories

Image 2.4: Scan the code to find supplemental resources for supporting Hack 2.

HACK 3

RENOVATE YOUR SPACE

Upcycling, rearranging, and repurposing your resources

When I organize my classroom as a workshop, the physical arrangement calls for motion. In turn, the organization of the workshop structures the motion and keeps it purposeful.
— NANCIE ATWELL, TEACHER, WRITER, AND WORKSHOP PIONEER

THE PROBLEM: WE DON'T PUT ENOUGH THOUGHT INTO SPACES FOR MAKING AND WRITING

FEW GROUPS OF students come together ready to work interdependently, but the space in which they meet can make a huge difference. We must create the environment where meaningful making and writing can happen.

My first workshop was an elementary classroom in a suburb of Buffalo, New York. During my tenure as a teacher in the years that ensued, I led workshops in public high schools, and I created a middle school writing workshop that ran beside the required eighth-grade English class (that I also taught for over a decade). Each time I designed these writing workshops, I gave only a tiny bit of thought to the space itself or the resources I invited writers to use. Instead, I focused on creating curriculum, designing rubrics, and gathering a mighty collection of mentor texts for my classroom library. I learned how to establish solid record-keeping practices, how to lead mini-lessons, and how to confer with writers (something I'm still getting better at).

I arranged the desks in groups that made for productive accountable talk and the occasional exchange of feedback. I kept a set of useful writing supplies in a separate corner of the room, and I established routines and rituals that helped my students make good use of the spaces that I created for mini-lessons, independent and collaborative work, and teacher and peer conferences. I bought and hung some lovely posters. I designed cute bulletin boards. That was really the full extent of my efforts to create meaningful space, though. If only I could turn back time, I would design those workshop spaces to be so much more engaging and inviting to my young makers and writers.

Designing a better environment for making and writing didn't seem like much of an option until I began creating writing studios outside of schools. My first experience with this began in 2008, when I opened the WNY Young Writers' Studio. Over the course of nine years, we took up space in three different buildings, including a large storefront and an even bigger classroom on the third floor of a former church school building. Each time we moved, we remade our space, improving on the one we left behind.

And now, when I lead Make Writing Pop-Up Studios in schools,

I'm offered access to spaces and a myriad of tools that are so much more dynamic. I'm not the only one who's learned that the spaces we create and the resources with which we fill them matter. This has been one of the greatest learnings of my career.

THE HACK: RENOVATE YOUR SPACE WITH A JUST-RIGHT DESIGN AND JUST-RIGHT TOOLS

Experience has taught me that making an ideal space takes time and patience. Now, every studio and makerspace that I design or work in evolves one layer at a time. The substructure of the space is typically prepared before we open our doors or launch a new year of learning. Once the kids arrive, our start-up begins: We assess their needs and interests, add a few more resources and adjust our space accordingly. Finally, as everyone begins pursuing unique projects, our tools become more specialized. I never hang a single poster inside of these new spaces, and inasmuch as possible, I leave the walls empty so they can become design boards for the kids.

Launching makerspaces for writers has taught me that abundance matters. When space, supplies, energy, support, acceptance, and respect are abundant, students are willing to take risks and make mistakes. They aren't afraid to throw things out. However, constraint matters too, and so the ideas that follow will help you foster a sense of abundance while establishing boundaries that prevent students from feeling overwhelmed.

> RECOGNIZE THE DIVERSE SKILL SET AND INCREDIBLE TALENT IN YOUR OWN FACULTY, AND SEEK OUT STUDENTS WHO ARE WILLING TO SHARE THEIR EXPERTISE WITH OTHERS.

You'll find additional ideas, photo tours of inspiring makerspaces and studios (including my own) in the supplemental

59

resources folder through the QR code at the end of this Hack. There, you will also find resource lists that can help you provide a healthy assortment of diverse materials to eager makers and writers without spending a fortune.

WHAT YOU CAN DO TOMORROW

If your space looks and functions more like a classroom than a studio or makerspace, you'll find the suggestions that follow particularly helpful. Hopefully they'll inspire you to start making swift but simple changes without investing too much time or money.

- **CREATE SIMPLE, PREDICTABLE, AND PURPOSEFUL SPACES.** Writers will need spaces to gather for lessons and shared learning, quiet places to write, collaborative spaces where they can make and confer, and centers that support focused inquiry. These might include libraries of diverse print materials, and technology tools that support searching, Skyping, and other ways of connecting with information and people around the globe.

  While many are enticed by the idea of moveable spaces, I've found that predictability matters. Writers and makers tend to stake claims on the spots where they're most comfortable working, and when kids know where to find things, they're more inclined to go looking for them independently. Studios and makerspaces aren't always aesthetically pleasing, either. So, rather than purchasing expensive furniture or filling your space with shiny, color-coordinated bins, consider rearranging, repurposing, and hacking what you already have.

The walls of writing makerspaces and studios are typically barren, save for the charts, sticky notes, and planning work of the creatives who use them. Kids use the walls to map out drafts, tinker with the loose parts of their texts, brainstorm, and problem-solve. Empty walls are inviting. Cute posters distract.

- **CREATE DELIGHTFUL DIVERSIONS.** We have a notebook nook in my writing studio, and a dress-up area, too. You may be surprised at the popularity of the break-it box, which is filled with defunct tech tools and small appliances that kids are welcome to take apart. We have a growing collection of board games for word nerds, and when I work with elementary writers, I like to make a sticky station where hot glue guns, staplers, tape, and similar tools reside. Having these items all in one place helps me keep a closer watch, so kids can make safely. It also facilitates sharing when supplies are expensive or few in number. How might you create spaces that serve as catalysts for creative writing and making?

Image 3.1: The notebook nook at the
WNY Young Writers' Studio

- **HELP KIDS ACCESS THE RIGHT TOOLS AT THE RIGHT TIME.** I've learned that when I provide abundant choices and wide-open access to every resource in the room, learners quickly become overwhelmed. When I set limits around what might be used and when, students' choices become more thoughtful, and their work becomes more purposeful and often, more complex. Consider why students are writing or making, the amount of time you have available for either of these endeavors, and what a successful outcome might look like. These answers will guide your decisions as you put tools and resources in front of students.

Quick challenges like firestarters don't require many maker tools or materials. In fact, the constraints provided within the challenge contribute to students' critical thinking and inspire creativity. It's enough to give kids a handful of loose parts that can be used in a bunch of different ways. I'll often tuck simple things like string, rubber bands, index cards, and binder clips into an envelope with the expectation that kids will repurpose them as they prototype.

I've also created tiny tinker totes, tinker trays, and tool buckets. I give totes to every writer in the room, but trays and tool buckets are shared by whole groups. At the WNY Young Writers' Studio, we fashioned a mobile makerspace out of an old storage shelf, reclaimed peg board, a piece of plywood, and a set of wheels. We attached the pegboard to the back of the shelf and hung all our small tools off of it. We stored tubs of paint, blocks, recyclables, paper, Legos, clay, and other larger supplies on the shelves. You'll see an example of a tote, tinker tray, and tool bucket in Image 3.2, and you'll find an entire blog post about our mobile makerspace in the supplemental resources file for this Hack.

Image 3.2: Tiny tinker totes, tinker trays, and tool buckets
invite writers to make with varied resources.

- **INVITE THEM TO BRING THEIR OWN STUFF.**
As writers consider how they might translate print
through new modalities and forms, ideas for perfected
projects begin to emerge, and their needs become
specialized. Typically, kids who are interested in producing perfected works of art in addition to print will
make choices that play to their interests and strengths,
and often, they'll already have some of what they
need to complete these pieces on hand. Invite them
to bring their own items to school.

- **PLAN YOUR STORAGE.** In addition to providing
spaces for making, writing, and collaboration, you will
want to plan for storage. Kids need places to keep
the things they build and a way to store loose parts
and other materials they are using. Some teachers are

fortunate enough to have ample shelf space, cubbies, and extra lockers. Many don't, though. Consider how you might create room for students to manage and protect their materials. I've gathered some ideas for you online. Scan the QR code for this Hack, and dive into the supplemental resources folder to learn more.

A BLUEPRINT FOR FULL IMPLEMENTATION

Step 1: Bring the outside in.

Bring the people and places and making and writing that are happening outside of your classroom into the classroom. Provide opportunities for your students to talk about the activities they're passionate about, and help them align their learning inside your space with their learning outside of it. Invite them to transform your space to make it more conducive to the kinds of creating they do outside of school.

Step 2: Encourage your students to step out.

If possible, allow your students to leave your room when they need to make and write elsewhere in the most fitting spaces. Practicing empathy often inspires students to seek out immersive experiences. Encourage this, create protocols for it, and provide models that your students can emulate. If you need examples and resources, follow the QR code to the supplemental resources folder for this Hack.

Step 3: Open your space.

Recognize the diverse skill set and incredible talent in your own faculty, and seek out students who are willing to share their expertise with others. Create opportunities for them to talk with your students formally and informally. Open your space to those who are willing to support your teaching through their examples or direct coaching. Do you know a teacher who designs websites? Give her a space in your room. What about a student artist who is storyboarding an exhibition? Invite him to do that in your workshop. I've met principals who build their own model railroads, high school teachers who love to garden, and first-graders who invented their own candy machines. Find out what people are making. Let them do it in your space. Your students will learn a lot from them, and you will too.

Step 4: Get everyone connected.

Encourage writers to use technology to build their own global learning networks. Let them design their own websites and create their own profiles inside spaces where others with similar interests in writing and making also hang out. Do this for yourself, and model it for your students. Communities thrive when members are connected to those outside of the bubble.

OVERCOMING PUSHBACK

Few teachers would argue against turning their classrooms into makerspaces for writers. I know that these kinds of changes rarely come easy, though. As I began drafting this Hack, I turned to my colleagues in the Building Better Writers Facebook group for perspective. They pushed my thinking hard when they shared their concerns.

I don't have my own space. There are ways to create opportunities for making, even if you're working in a shared space, or even teaching off a cart. Consider filling a tool bucket with loose parts and supplies, send your students out more often than inviting others in, and treat each form as a build that can be broken into loose parts. We'll explore this further in Hack 7.

My administrators won't support this. Share this book, and ask if you might test these ideas through a light action research project. Ask if you can try some of these approaches with your most resistant writers first. See if you can make writing through just one unit. Perhaps you can try, if you document and share your findings along the way. And if the answer is still no, then ask why not? Especially if the traditional approaches that you've been required to use aren't moving writers forward as effectively as you'd like.

My students will want to keep everything they make! I don't have the room. Unless writers are creating perfected works of art beside their print pieces, the making that happens inside of workshop typically generates low-res prototypes. Help students understand up front that prototypes aren't precious. They don't look like anything we'd keep. They're typically made from inexpensive materials and loose parts that have been repurposed. Prototyping isn't pretty; it's ideation and experimentation—thinking and tinkering and learning to elevate writing. Once we've discovered what we need to move our process and our writing forward, we take those prototypes apart. We let them go. When kids insist on keeping prototypes, I suggest they snap photos or take them home. When they create perfected works of art beside their manuscripts, they're expected to share both pieces with real audiences. Create enough storage for makers to keep their works in progress, but make it clear that space is limited and builds must move through your space rather than residing there indefinitely.

This is going to be too expensive. Recycling bins, craft closets, and junk drawers hold unimaginable treasures. Before you go shopping, take inventory of what you already have on hand. Then, let parents and colleagues know what you might need. Many will be happy to donate gently used items and scrap materials that were destined for the trash. Remember, prototyping isn't arts and crafts. Repurposing IS the purpose, and the aesthetic doesn't matter as much as the intention behind the design. Use what you must let kids rapidly prototype in order to elevate their writing. Those who commit to producing perfected works of art will often be willing to bring in their own materials. As your space evolves, you'll be better able to prioritize your budget and seek out other sources of funding, too. When this isn't possible, engage makers in a bit of problem-solving: How can we stay under budget? This is an authentic challenge that most creatives face. Let them work through it inside your workshop.

THE HACK IN ACTION

How might you co-design your space along with the writers and makers it will serve? This question became a stone in my shoe in the spring of 2012 as I prepared to open a new writing studio in my home town of Kenmore, New York. At the time, I'd been writing and making with teachers and kids consistently for about five years. We met on college campuses, in local community rooms, and for a long time, in the library and adjoining computer lab in Union East Elementary School in Cheektowaga, New York. When a little storefront became available five blocks from my house, my husband finally convinced me: It was time to make a studio home of our own.

I didn't want to fill the space ahead of anyone's arrival. Instead, I wanted to create a collaborative vision for how our studio would look, and more importantly, how it would function. I mailed invitations, ordered a cake, and my husband made a ton of food. Kids and teachers and parents arrived. I made them a party, and I gave them the space. This was my gift to them all.

I lined the walls with chart paper and a variety of pointed prompts:

How might we make the best use of this space?
How might we arrange it in a way that will feed our learning and work?
What does your ideal creative space look like? How does it function? What's present there? What's missing? Why?
What will we NEED to make this space useful? What do we WANT? How should we go about getting these things? What will your contribution be?
How will we care for this space?

In addition to these questions, I provided a variety of tools: markers and paint and pencils and crayons, devices that allowed everyone a peek at similar sorts of spaces, magazines and newspapers and other print material that inspired our space designers to share their ideas via collage, and every single book I could get my hands on that said anything about creating spaces for creative people. Partygoers dove in, ideated, and prototyped all over the chart paper that hung on the walls. I used their recommendations to create a shared vision for our space, and then we made an action plan to make it a reality.

I didn't do this work alone—kids helped with the build. Nearly every bit of furniture was reclaimed, upcycled, and hacked. I spent as little as possible. We bought only the most basic materials and resources, knowing that once our writing and making began, the space would evolve even further. And it did.

As another example, I'd like to tell you about Courtney Bryant,

STEAM Project Manager and Engineering Design Resident Coordinator at Charles R. Drew Charter School in Atlanta, Georgia. She was eager to inspire making without overcrowding classrooms or wasting resources. Her solution? STEAM Trunks.

"These mobile makerspaces are on the move daily," she said. "They make hands-on learning possible." On a walk through her school, one might find a student soldering a circuit together using the Electronics Trunk or using the 3D Printer Trunk to make pieces for puppets they've created to activate a script they wrote in Spanish class. Students design and build sets for plays they've written using the Construction Trunk, too.

"The trunks provide students real-world tools to solve real-world problems within the space of traditional classrooms," Courtney explained. "Having the trunks available for teachers means that we are able to share resources and teachers need not crowd their rooms with tools and supplies that are not in use at the time."

Teachers receive training on how to use the trunks as they are needed for projects, and they reserve the trunks through an online form. Trunks are delivered at the appointed date and time, fully stocked and ready to go.

"Each trunk has a personality all its own," Courtney continued. "Students were asked to create a cart they would get excited to see rolling down the hall. The response was overwhelming. Kids are still awestruck whenever the carts move through the halls. They stop and stare with longing faces—hoping the carts turn into their room. Even our high school students love the trunks. I've watched them roll into their literature classes—instant engagement."

Drew Charter School was designed for transparency and interactivity. The buildings were made with a lot of interior glass for several reasons: Everyone can see students working in groups as they move throughout the buildings, the glass serves as another writing surface for students in every classroom, and most importantly, everyone can see how students tackle their learning inside of this community.

"Our students routinely write on the glass walls and tables in our classrooms," Courtney said. "Their work is on display for all to see. In the Senior Academy, several classrooms on each floor are made with collapsible walls so that teachers and entire classes can collaborate. We also have Project Based Learning labs that were created so that students could move from their traditional classroom space into a larger more open space whenever they're designing large-scale installations or conducting investigations that demand more space."

How a studio looks is not nearly as important as how it functions. So, even if your current environment consists of four barren walls and antiseptic furnishings, small shifts in how you arrange your space and repurpose your resources will ensure that the workshop becomes a studio—or as others call it, a makerspace—for writers.

Take a trip to the supplemental resources folder for this Hack by scanning the image below. Share the ideas with your students. Then, throw your own design party, and share the plans that emerge in the #MakeWriting stream on Twitter. Here's what you'll find inside:

- Examples of inspiring makerspaces, writing workshops, and studios

- A blog post about our mobile makerspace at the WNY Young Writers' Studio

- Protocols for immersive experiences

Image 3.3: Scan the code to find supplemental resources for supporting Hack 3.

HACK 4

CREATE A WRITER-CENTERED WORKSHOP

Fostering compassion, collective expertise, and collaboration

Cultures are never merely intellectual constructs. They take form through the collective intelligence and memory, through a commonly held psychology and emotions, through spiritual and artistic communion.
— TARIQ RAMADAN, PHILOSOPHER AND WRITER

THE PROBLEM: WRITING WORKSHOPS ARE TOO TEACHER-CENTERED

CONSTRUCTIVISM, THE THEORY that learning is best accomplished by doing, fuels a maker culture. While immersive experiences like apprenticeships engage those with do-it-yourself dispositions, embracing learner-centered models has other positive effects as well. A major one is the cultivation of inter-dependence. This is what distinguishes makerspaces, studios, and true learning communities from traditional classrooms and workshops.

The thing about constructivism that I find so appealing is that it makes learning transparent, not merely the product of it. Makers share, and that spirit of generosity grows their collective intelligence. This helps them get better at what they do. Generosity promotes and sustains their progress, and it also diminishes shame. When everyone is making, everyone is struggling, failing, and persevering ... in front of each other. Over time, this has the potential to change our beliefs about learning, succeeding, and what it means to be of value inside of a community.

Often, our workshops are designed and directed by teachers who take tremendous ownership and pride in what they do. And well they should, as their talent is often as great as their intentions. The pull of teachers inside traditional workshops can undermine interdependence, though. They create a sort of gravity that can draw learners away from one another and toward the front of the room, where they alone hold the mentor texts and all the expertise. Too often, students slide into orbit like planets to their sun.

It's no wonder that so many writers struggle to take initiative. It's no wonder that many completely disengage.

THE HACK: CREATE A WRITER-CENTERED WORKSHOP

In a writer-centered workshop, teachers create frameworks, protocols, and conditions for learning, but they take a less directive role in leading it. They're facilitators, and they're connectors, too. They recognize that interdependence is a critical component of the future-ready workshop, and they build it with intention. They know that the writer-centered culture they create will help young students learn and work together better, and that it will prepare them to learn and work in a future world that is very different from the one in which their teachers grew up.

Interdependence is cultivated inside of communities that deliberately pursue shared expertise, and the norms that we establish in our workshops may strengthen or undermine these efforts. Making a handful of adaptations to traditional writing workshop expectations, routines, and procedures has the potential to increase levels of interdependence. Coaching the development of certain dispositions does as well, and when teachers become mindful of the behaviors they're modeling, every writer within the community shifts in response. This requires us to think about more than curriculum, instruction, and assessment. How we attend to each writer's well-being matters, and the more human we are, the better.

It helps to begin with a clear set of expectations. These are the ones I often share as new writing communities begin to take shape. I'm honest about the fact that this manifesto emerged from my vision, and I welcome writers to make additions and adjustments as needed. It's a starting point, and it always evolves.

- Find purposes that matter to you, and help others do the same for themselves.

- Take risks, generate a lot of ideas, and keep them safe for future use.

- Commit. Be decisive.

- Work toward conventionality.

- Put people before products. Help them move forward, so they can move their work forward.

- Figure out how you will matter to this community. Contribute. Make a mark.

- Show gratitude.

- Take good care of your space and the people in it.

Once we're aligned to a shared vision, the harder work begins: putting our intentions into practice.

WHAT YOU CAN DO TOMORROW

The content we teach, the skills we coach, and the processes through which we move writers all have forms that make them feel more tangible. To many, what's tangible is what's real, and so shaping culture often seems intangible and much more challenging. It's elusive; invisible. Or so we think.

The ideas that follow can help you begin to construct a culture of interdependent, compassionate, and open-minded thinkers, writers, and tinkerers.

- **CONSIDER YOUR ROUTINES AND PROCEDURES.**
  Routines are the things that we do with regularity inside of our workshops. Common routines include setting up and cleaning up from firestarter challenges, transitioning from one space in the room

to another, signaling that it's time to meet, meeting for shared mini-lessons, practicing active listening, turning to talk to partners or group members, gathering the materials we need, storing builds, requesting conferences, and writing even while we're waiting for help or direction. You'll find my resources for supporting routine building in the supplemental folder for this Hack.

> WHEN WE CREATE THEORIES OF CHANGE FOR OUR MOVES TO WRITER-CENTERED WORKSHOPS, WE DEFINE OUR ULTIMATE VISION, INTENDED OUTCOMES, ALIGNED INPUTS, ACTIVITIES, AND INTENDED IMPACT.

Take some time to consider the unintended consequences of your well-intended routines and procedures. As you begin assessing what you currently do or begin planning for the first time, consider how you will frame and possibly reframe your routines and procedures to foster interdependence and collaboration. The ideas outlined in Image 4.1 offer inspiration.

Routines that Foster Interdependence

Routines that Welcome Writers and Makers into the Workshop

Explore the space one area at a time. Facilitate shared decision-making:

How did the designer intend for the space to be used?

How might the users improve upon the design?

How will each space and the tools in it be cared for? Who will care for it? When?

Explore the structure of the workshop session. Reach consensus:

How will we structure our time, so that we might learn from one another, work independently, and make time to reflect and plan?

Where will we meet for each kind of learning, writing, and making? Why?

Which resources and materials will we use when?

Where will resources and materials be kept?

How will we speak?

How will we listen?

How will we show people we are hearing them?

What will we do when we don't feel heard?

How will we move from one place to another without disrupting others' learning?

Routines that Cultivate Collaboration

Introduce protocols in order to ensure equity in each of these situations:

*You will find examples in the supplemental resources folder for this hack.

Accountable talk

Peer review

Learning from work samples

Learning from mentor texts

Inquiry

Resolving dilemmas

Celebrating writing

Sharing expertise

Routines that Sustain Independent Writing and Making

Prompt writers to reflect on these questions and create work plans:

What do I hope to learn today? Who will I learn from? When? How?

What do I hope to produce today? How will I produce it? When? How?

How will I plan my time and use my resources in order to have a satisfying session?

How might I get stuck? Which tools will help me? Which writers will?

When does it make sense to ask for help? How will I do this?

How will I manage my work? My materials?

How will I manage my frustration?

Figure 4.1: Reframing routines and procedures

- **SELECT THE VALUES, HABITS, AND BELIEFS THAT WILL GUIDE YOUR TEACHING.** First, you will want to intentionally define the specific values, habits, and beliefs that you hope to grow in your students. Some turn to the work of other experts for this, as there are several frameworks and models that define character strengths and dispositions. In my own work with young writers, I rely on the Dispositions of Practice, defined by Communities for Learning, Leading Lasting Change. I know many who value Art Costa and Bena Kallick's Habits of Mind as well, and my colleague, Ellen Feig Gray, often uses the Values in Action (VIA) Character Strengths when she collaborates with me and other educators. (See more about Ellen's VIA work in the Hack in Action section later in this chapter.)

Image 4.2: Students from Chappaqua Central School District engage in strength spotting using the VIA Character Strengths.

These frameworks have much in common. Perhaps you prefer another that you've already made your own. In my experience, *how* we use the framework is just as important as *which* framework we choose. How do you define and model the values, habits, and beliefs that you want your students to engender? How do you help them spot their strengths? How do you help them recognize the strengths that their peers possess? While many use frameworks like these for self-assessment and goal setting, I prefer to take an appreciative inquiry approach whenever I'm helping students notice, name, and grow the good in themselves and others. You'll find resources that will help you do the same by dropping into the supplemental resources folder for this Hack.

- **SHINE A SPOTLIGHT ON EXPERTISE.** Rather than zooming in on each writer's needs, take time to help them notice and name their areas of expertise. It's important that each writer define precisely what he or she is good at, and it's even more important that the rest of the room takes notice of the skills of others. We help writers build collective expertise when we push pause on independent work time long enough to shine a spotlight on something unexpected that someone is doing well. We build collective expertise when we invite writers to demonstrate a craft move, a maker move, a strategy, or a solution they've discovered so the rest of the class might benefit from their wisdom. We build collective expertise when we turn writers toward one another when they struggle, rather than making them dependent on us for intervention.

  A final word: Expertise is something that we must showcase every day if we're to create an interdependent community. If we wait for formal celebrations, presentations, or assemblies to recognize the contributions that writers make to our collective, this practice will feel more like a novelty and kids will likely interpret it as a congratulatory gesture. Make time to let expertise shine on the daily. When you do, kids will stop relying on you, and that's a good thing.

Image 4.3: Students end a writing workshop
session by exhibiting newfound skills.

- **REFRAME YOUR ROLE AND REDEFINE YOUR WORK.** As a learning facilitator, your role involves creating the conditions for learning, noticing when it is happening, investigating why and how, and amplifying it so others can benefit. Start to intentionally notice when the time is right to share your own expertise—particularly during mini-lessons where you are helping students strive toward new learning targets. Also, become more aware when your work should involve watching learners, documenting their expertise, and ensuring that others gain access to it. I share practical ways to begin and sustain this work in the supplemental resources folder for this Hack.

A BLUEPRINT FOR FULL IMPLEMENTATION

Step 1: Create a theory of change.

A theory of change is a comprehensive map of how and when a specific change is expected to happen. When we create theories of change for our moves to writer-centered workshops, we define our ultimate vision, intended outcomes, aligned inputs, activities, and intended impact. Theories of change can help us prioritize the values, beliefs, and habits we hope to cultivate, the work we will do to accomplish this, understandings of what success looks like, and a timeline for executing the change. They're powerful and dynamic tools that offer coherence and structure to complex processes. You will see examples of theories of cultural change in the supplemental resources folder for this Hack.

Step 2: Engage the entire system.

Consider how you will begin to share the cultural shifts occurring inside of your writing workshop with school leaders and staff members who work outside of it. Think about what might happen if you don't share. In my experience, kids who become increasingly interdependent in workshop often find themselves misunderstood in other settings. Tensions arise when they practice the same values in other contexts, especially when teachers do not position themselves as facilitators of learning, but instead, as directors and evaluators who expect compliance. I believe that those who work to create significant cultural shifts inside of one part of a system have a responsibility to invite everyone else along and to help kids respectfully advocate for themselves when necessary. The unintended consequences can be great when we stay quiet.

Step 3: Assess cultural progress over time.

Theories of change help us identify powerful assessment moments within an initiative. While students might reflect on their growing character strengths inside of writers' notebooks and during conferences with you, you might gather other evidence of change—and those who are supporting you within the system can do the same. Determine which evidence is best to collect, when you will collect it, and how it will be used. Assessing cultural progress over time creates agile changemakers. You'll find examples of this work in the theories of change materials included in the supplemental resources folder for this hack.

OVERCOMING PUSHBACK

The greatest pushback teachers often encounter when fostering interdependence is their own. It's difficult to relinquish control, watch students struggle, and perhaps discover that we've been doing some things wrong all along. The following concerns are common. I have provided my best answers, but you can determine how you will best overcome them.

These skills are so soft that I'm uncertain how to create accountability. Accountability in the form of grades, rewards, or punishment doesn't do much to build interdependence. These things foster competitiveness, and often, they incite shame. The kind of accountability that will enable the growth of interdependence is in the form of developing character and enriching the culture of the entire community. It sets a precedent and a tone. When we refuse to engage negativity but instead, notice and leverage every learner's strengths, it grows the good inside of a community. And when we respond to disengagement with curiosity and genuine support, we often discover what's needed to bring everyone along.

My students seem to resent investing time and energy in work that has nothing to do with writing. This can be uncomfortable work for those who have never done it before. Many writers have never been invited to define and share their character strengths. Some have been taught to confuse confidence with arrogance. Others feel it might be disrespectful to claim the floor. That's where the teacher does her magic, after all. It's not uncommon for kids to resist this kind of learning, and that's only more evidence of how critical it is. Start small and move slowly, but make this a part of every day in your workshop. By year-end, you'll be amazed by the results.

The culture in my workshop is so different from the ones my students encounter in other classes, and this is causing tension. It often will. Sometimes, students will carry your classroom vision and values into other spaces that function differently. Sometimes, the leaders of those spaces won't understand or appreciate them, either. Students who haven't had the opportunity to learn with you may challenge the kids who have. Your students may be challenged by the cultures they encounter elsewhere. How will you handle each of these scenarios? Perhaps you'll recognize yourself or your students in the first Hack in Action example that follows. Or perhaps you'd rather talk about all this a bit more. Look for me @AngelaStockman on Twitter. We can chat.

THE HACK IN ACTION

I remember the first time one of my writers found herself grappling with what I've come to recognize as a sort of culture shock. This is common when kids who have been coached to become interdependent find themselves inside of a classroom whose leader is decidedly authoritarian.

We'd been writing together throughout the morning when she came to me and quietly asked if we could chat after all the other kids had gone home. I noticed that she seemed nervous, and it wasn't characteristic of her.

"What's up?" I asked, closing the door behind the last writer to leave.

"Do you remember how I set a goal last summer to finish writing an entire novel?" she asked, and of course I remembered. I smiled brightly and said, "That was quite an accomplishment."

"Yeah," she bit her lip, taking a long look out the window. "About that." As she tried to continue, tears began to form in her eyes. "So, I was really excited to take creative writing at school this year," she told me. "I know the teacher is well-respected. He's a very talented writer himself. In fact, he really intimidates me."

I nodded. "Go on."

"Well, I asked him to give me feedback on my manuscript, and he kept it for a while. Then, when we finally met, he told me that maybe if I stayed after school every day for this entire year and spent even more time revising it, I might be able to publish it. He said it didn't show much promise."

My heart broke. The writers that I support are trained to provide quality feedback to one another. This is hard learning. It takes time. It also takes a great deal of empathy. Many of the kids that I write with provide better feedback than the adults I know. This writer was one of the best.

I was hurt for her, because she spent so much time improving her writing and serving other kids in our community who always wanted her feedback. I was also furious with her teacher, who I knew fairly well. I wanted to tell her that truly talented writers never tear others down. I wanted to tell her that he was wrong and that she could publish her writing that very day if she wanted to. I wanted to tell her to complain to her principal and to ask her mother to call the guidance department to switch her out of his class.

I wanted to say so many, many things in that moment, but instead I nodded and quietly asked, "How did you advocate for yourself?"

She looked confused.

"I'm serious," I said sternly, looking her dead in the eyes. "How did you advocate for yourself?"

"I'm not sure what you mean," she stammered, scanning the floor and the walls, as if the answer was waiting there.

"Well, as I understand it, you asked your teacher to provide you feedback," I told her. "Did you ask for his evaluation? Did you ask his opinion on whether your work was ready for publication?"

She shook her head. "No," I validated her. "You did not. Here's the thing, though—it's not uncommon for people to confuse feedback with evaluation. Maybe you should try again. Maybe if you're clearer about what you need, he'll be able to help you better."

"Maybe," she wiped her cheek.

"How will you do it?" I asked, inviting her to rehearse the exchange.

"Well, I could give him our peer review protocol and ask him to use that instead of his own opinions," she offered, and I told her this was a great idea. I asked her how she would request this from her teacher in a way that wouldn't offend him.

"I'll just tell him that we use it here, in our writing studio, and it helps me a lot," she told me. "I'll ask him if he minds using it when he talks with me about my writing." This seemed respectful. She would ask if he might use the protocol that helped her, and she would also make it clear that she respected his right to refuse.

"What if he says no?" she asked, horror washing over her face again.

"Then, you need to find someone who is better able to provide you the feedback you need," I smiled. "It's your work. You're responsible for making these choices. It's hard to find good people to review our writing. We get better at knowing who to ask—and when—over time."

When we met again a few weeks later, she was glowing. "He really liked the protocol," she told me. "In fact, he started using it with all of us in class."

This didn't surprise me at all. "It's how you handled yourself," I told her, and then I said that her courage and willingness to own and share her expertise made me proud.

When we create learning cultures that are vastly different from the ones our colleagues maintain, it's likely that some may not handle things so well, and that's okay. In fact, it's better than okay if this provides our students opportunities to practice strength-spotting and self-advocacy. These are important life skills.

Finding the words for what we're good at can be challenging, though, and without those words, strength-spotting is almost impossible. This is why it's so important to create or adopt a framework that makes character strengths explicit. My colleague, Ellen Feig Gray, is a research psychologist and certified positive psychology practitioner who relies on the VIA Character Strengths for this purpose.

During the summer of 2017, Ellen accompanied me as I led Make Writing Pop-Up Studio sessions in upstate New York. This is where we met Calvin, an incredibly resistant but equally gifted young writer. Calvin spent the first days of our week-long intensive out of his seat, climbing up on tables, and swinging from any stable surface that would support him. We learned a great deal by watching him, and this helped me ask better questions. Calvin had a certain dry wit that many exceptionally resistant but talented writers tend to carry around. Initially, he refused to write, but he would build anything, and when I interviewed him about the things he was making and the ideas that were emerging, his story lines were rich and coherent. They were also a bit more provocative than most could conceive of at his age.

My younger self would have struggled with Calvin. I would have maintained a hard line around the rules, intervened every time he got out of his seat, and nagged him about using print. Back then I never devoted time to naming and noticing character strengths. It occurs to me now that when we fail to do this, kids tend to focus on flaws—their own and everyone else's. This is no way to build community.

"Our brains are hardwired for negativity," Ellen reminded me. "We're protective creatures, so we tend to focus on what could go wrong and what needs to be fixed instead of what's right and whole."

I kept this in mind during every exchange with Calvin. Rather than reacting to his negative attention-seeking behaviors or ignoring them altogether, I found something legitimate to validate about his behavior or the values it was reflecting. Calvin learned best when he was moving. He was tenacious with his builds. Calvin was clever, funny, and well-read. "I love mythology," he confided in me one day. "I really wish we could have spent more time in the library."

Calvin was an asset to our workshop community, and it was thanks to Ellen that the rest of the kids recognized this as well. During our first days together, I spent time introducing the Values in Action Character Strengths. Kids wandered the room, exploring brightly colored cards that defined each of the strengths in a language they could understand. They looked for themselves there, selecting their own strengths and sharing them with everyone else in the class.

Calvin was hesitant to participate. So we took a risk and invited the class to define the strengths they saw in Calvin. Ellen explained that this sort of strength-spotting is not only empowering for kids like Calvin, it helps to establish a positive, interdependent culture.

That morning, Calvin learned that others saw his good humor. They noticed how he approached each task with zest. They affirmed that he was creative, and he was persevering. He had a contribution to make.

From that moment forward, Calvin approached his work with newfound respect, and everyone in the room treated him with it as well.

As writers begin to notice, name, and mindfully grow their character strengths, reflection becomes a critical part of the process. Writers' notebooks provide a container for this work, enabling students to document what they're noticing about themselves and the entire community as everyone gains more experience and becomes increasingly interdependent. The next Hack will provide a peek into a notebook system and tools that can help ensure meaningful, daily use. Before you jump ahead, take some time to explore the supplemental resources for this Hack. They include:

- Examples of routines and procedures for maker-spaces, workshops, and studios

- Resources for practicing appreciative inquiry

- Ideas that will help students name and share their expertise

- Theories of change

Image 4.4: Scan the code to find supplemental resources for supporting Hack 4.

HACK 5
BUILD A BETTER NOTEBOOK
Ensuring consistent use

Cheap paper is less perishable than gray matter, and
lead pencil markings endure longer than memory.
— Jack London, Author

THE PROBLEM: THE EMPTY OR
UNDERDEVELOPED NOTEBOOK

A NOTEBOOK CAN BECOME a writer's greatest tool. Unlike a journal, where we engage in freewriting, a notebook is a container for ideas that we may or may not use: critical content and strategies that we learn from lessons or research, experimental bits of drafts, our attempts to write like others, and reflections on our thinking, learning, and growth.

In my experience, when teachers help writers organize and use their notebooks with deliberate intention, their writers' lives and the work they produce are greater for it. When they don't, writers often struggle to find or sustain their purposes for notebook keeping. Books go home empty at the end of each year, and teachers and kids alike fail to reach their fullest potential.

I've never met a teacher or a writer who wasn't inspired by the idea of notebook keeping, but I've met many who struggle to find the time to use them well inside of the classroom. Even writers with the best of intentions find themselves abandoning their notebooks as other expectations and demands dominate their writing time. When notebook keeping is treated as an additional task inside of the workshop or studio, it quickly becomes a "may do" rather than a "must do."

Let's design a notebook—for ourselves and our students—that is essential to our writing lives.

THE HACK: BUILD A BETTER NOTEBOOK

What works for me may not work for you or for your students. You're welcome to replicate this approach, and you'll find plenty of supporting tools in the supplemental resources folder for this Hack, but your own process may prove far more beneficial to you in the end. These are the questions I ask myself as I improve notebook keeping practices with the writers I support:

1. Why does my workshop or studio matter?

2. Ideally, what will writers know and be able to do as a result of learning with me?

3. How will they learn and do these things?

4. How might I work with my students to create a notebook structure that enables this vision and fuels all efforts to achieve it?

My students study writing and writers: What makes them influential and what we can learn from them. We strive to improve process, craft, and the growth of certain dispositions. We do this inside of studios and makerspaces by using the design thinking process. Our notebook structure must help writers accomplish this, so we've organized it accordingly. We have sections for:

- Idea-keeping

- Notes

- Tinkering and experimentation

- Self-assessment and reflection

I find the sections helpful, because I ask writers to revisit their thinking, learning, and work often. Our structure helps them find what they're looking for. It also helps them use their notebooks independently as a tool. What happens within each section might be highly experimental, but structuring our notebooks around our greater purposes reinforces what matters, allows us to apply what we've learned independently, and helps us assess our progress well.

NOTEBOOK KEEPERS ARE BRILLIANT PEOPLE, AND THEY'RE OFTEN VERY GENEROUS, TOO.

WHAT YOU CAN DO TOMORROW

I offer a few simple steps that you can adopt or adapt to ensure that your notebooks become treasured resources for your students:

- **CHOOSE YOUR TOOLS.** Decide who will choose the type of notebook for the class—you or your students. Consider the benefits and challenges of letting them choose. Then decide between analog or digital notebooks. If notebooks will be made of paper, select the best paper tool: spiral notebooks, composition books, handmade books, or something else. If you go with digital notebooks, find a powerful notebook-keeping tool online. Prepare to share these options with your students.

- **CREATE A NOTEBOOK STRUCTURE THAT REFLECTS YOUR GREATER PURPOSES.** My students' notebooks include sections for idea-keeping, notes, tinkering, and reflection because these align to our greater purposes. Writers make notes every day during our mini-lessons and while they are researching. They generate and keep ideas for their builds and drafts, and while they don't draft in their notebooks, they do experiment there. The tinkering section gives them a place to rewrite small sections of their drafts over and over again, trying different approaches and iterating until they're satisfied. Then, they drop their revision back into their drafts. We reflect daily at the end of each session. This section of our notebooks provides a container for this. To customize your own workshop notebooks, ask yourself these two questions: What are your greatest purposes as a teacher of writing? What do your students need from a notebook to develop as writers? When the sections of the notebook align to your greater purposes that drive your teaching and writing, the notebook becomes a meaningful tool. If you're interested in learning more about how my sections are designed and used, drop into the supplemental resources folder at the end of this Hack.

- **COACH WRITERS TO CREATE INSPIRING NOTEBOOK COVERS.** When I devote a mini-lesson to the creation of notebook covers, the students create far more inspiring results. Challenge kids to think about their favorite books, films, and songs. Invite them to locate quotes that they love. Give them permission to sketch images of people, places, and things that inspire them. Allow them to add photographs of those they love. Encourage the use of diverse mediums. Define options on a chart, so they remember what's possible. Add to your chart when kids share different but equally inspired ideas with you. See Image 5.1 for an example anchor chart that guides writers to create purposeful notebook covers. You'll find additional photos of my charts and example notebook covers in the supplemental resources folder for this Hack.

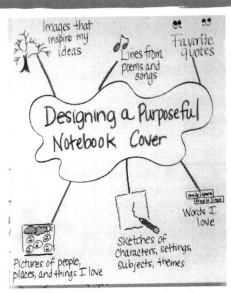

Image 5.1: An anchor chart defines the
criteria for inspiring notebook covers.

- **INSPIRE OWNERSHIP.** Many teachers find it valuable to reserve a portion of the notebook for whimsical use. Writers and makers choose how to use
  this portion of their notebook, and they share their
  approaches with others to inspire them. This builds
  ownership, and so does the keeping of a home notebook. I do this myself, and I share my home notebook
  with my students. My home notebook is just for me.
  I fill it however I want, with whatever I want, and I
  don't worry about keeping it in any kind of order. My
  workshop notebooks are sectioned and organized,
  and this helps me find important information, ideas,
  and reflections quickly when needed. My workshop
  notebook is a tool, and I keep it sharp. My home
  notebook is a sandbox, and I play in it.

A BLUEPRINT FOR FULL IMPLEMENTATION

Step 1: Use the notebook as evidence of what's most essential in your workshop.

At least a few times a year, I scan through writing notebooks and take note of those sections that get the most play and how writers are using them. This helps me understand which of my purposes tend to have the greatest priority inside of my workshop. It helps me reflect on how we're documenting and reflecting on our learning most often, too. Notebooks are powerful artifacts. They contain data that matters.

Image 5.2: Notebooks contain data that matters!

Step 2: Help writers use notebooks to lead more meaningful conferences.

I try to provide feedback to most writers every day. Our conferences are quick, and they happen at their workstations as I peer over their shoulders and into their work. I also meet with students as they prepare test prototypes and revise their work. These conferences typically take a tiny bit longer, and we sit together to talk things through. The third kind of conference is all about the writer—not the work. Here, we talk about our aligned vision, our growth together and separately as learners, how the community is evolving, and the writer's contribution to all of this. These conversations are far more revealing and rewarding when writers take the time to review notebook entries first. Prompting them helps. You'll find my writing conference prompts and protocols in the supplemental folder for this Hack.

Step 3: Connect to notebook mentors.

Notebook keepers are brilliant people, and they're often very generous, too. I keep an eye out for those who share their practices and tools online, and I introduce my writers to them. Teacher, poet, and author Amy Ludwig VanDerwater maintains a blog called Sharing Our Notebooks. Some of the writers I've supported over the years are featured there, along with many others. It's a beautiful resource to share with notebook keepers of all ages, and Amy welcomes guest posts, too.

OVERCOMING PUSHBACK

When notebooks are treated as ancillary tools, it can be difficult to use them in purposeful ways. Here are common challenges that prevent teachers from inviting notebook use, and a few thoughts on overcoming them:

We don't have time to keep notebooks. Then don't keep them... integrate them. Make sure that the notebook is a container for the most critical information, thinking, and experimentation that happens in your workshop. Make it a valuable place to store the artifacts of awesome, unforgettable experiences, rather than an added assignment to complete.

Notebooks aren't supposed to be structured. What if notebooks are supposed to be whatever they need to be in order to inspire writers and elevate their work? Prioritizing inspiration over elevation often undermines the process of notebook-keeping, in my experience. Structure often provides the kind of constraint that breeds creativity. In the absence of it, I've found that our notebooks remain unused.

Kids use their notebooks inconsistently. When we share a consistent invitation to use notebooks, students often use their notebooks more consistently. Try reminding writers when to use their notebooks throughout each session, using prompts like these:

> Please join me on the carpet for our mini-lesson, and turn your notebooks to the notes section.

> Writers, let's reflect on this prompt in our notebooks.

> I'm wondering how playing with the order of events might change your story. Tinker with the story map three different ways in your notebook.

> While you're waiting for our session to begin, make a list of all the injustices currently at work in your world. Build it in the ideas section of your notebook.

THE HACK IN ACTION

Akron Elementary teacher Kathryn (Kathy) Zbrzezny is an art journaler who photographs and shares the pages of her notebook with followers on Instagram. She also shares them with her second-grade students. Her enthusiasm for notebook-keeping is contagious, and her ideas are utterly sublime. In the fall of 2017, I spoke with Kathy about her passion for paper and ink. While her notebooks aren't structured, they are whimsical and inspired, and her daily discipline motivates her students.

"I've kept notebooks since I was nine years old," she told me. "I have composition books, diaries, journals, and art journals. When I was a child, I kept notebooks as a way to tell everything to 'someone'. My notebooks were my best listeners."

Kathy loved the act of writing and the notion that she could make her thoughts permanent. "I go back and read what I've written, long after the moments and those thoughts and feelings are gone. I've always been very much aware of the passage of time. Even as a child, I felt a need to capture moments and memories, and later, my thoughts, too." As an adult, she continues to keep notebooks because it gives her time to simply be herself, in the moment, and it relaxes her.

"I need to write," she explained. "Writing is my reflection and my release. I do it for myself." As a shy, introverted person, Kathy finds it easier to write than to speak. She's very private, but ironically, she's compelled to share her notebook pages on social media. "My process isn't complete until I connect with others. My private thoughts and written words are full of movement and motion. When I close them up inside of a notebook, everything stops. I feel an enormous release and connection when I share my notebook pages with others. This is how I tell my story."

Even as Kathy connects to other notebook-keepers globally, she fosters connections around notebooks in her classroom as well. There, notebooks are a powerful way for students to learn about themselves and one another. Kathy explained that this creates understanding and empathy, and notebooks not only improve student learning, but they also improve students' attitudes about learning.

"I begin dropping little hints that I love reading and writing and journals on the very first day of school," Kathy revealed. "I tell my second-graders that I have been writing in notebooks since I was their age, and this intrigues them. Soon enough, they will start asking me to bring my notebooks to school. When we sit down together on the rug, and I begin to open the page spreads, the excitement builds. My pages have colorful inks, washi tapes, doodles, and drawings. While I don't let them read all the words, I hold up my notebook and tell them what motivated and inspired my pages. This seems to be powerful—understanding that writing and drawing are motivated by something inside of me or my response to where I am and what I see and do. Children connect with this."

Her colleague, Hailey Barmasse, agreed. "I appreciate structured notebooks," she told me, "but I want my students to have space to write long." Hailey's purpose is to build her students' stamina for writing, and her notebooks help her achieve this goal. "They know that they can write about whatever they want whenever they want inside of their notebooks, but they have to write consistently, and they have to write long." This work happens beside the shared studies that students make of specific forms in Hailey's workshop.

"We make time for choice-based writing every week, and writers know that when they have a free moment at any time during the day, they're welcome to write in their notebooks." The element of choice has had a profound effect on students' motivation. "So does the fact that I'm pretty hands-off about things like spelling, punctuation, and mechanics," Hailey explained as she flipped through one of her students' notebooks to find examples of his willingness to take new risks with words. "He's spelled this one wrong, but he's using it," she smiles. "I love their inventive spelling."

She's learned how much her students love graphic novels and comic strips. This is much of what she finds inside of their notebooks. They tinker with design quite a bit, too. They are thoughtful about the images they include and where they place them. In one example, a student cut a portion of a top page away to expose the image on the page that followed it. It is inspiring to see this intention to delight, and willingness to experiment with traditional forms of writing to create something that readers don't typically see. It's what distinguishes future-ready writers from proficient ones.

If you'd like to see samples of this work, pages from Kathy's notebooks, or learn more about the art journalers that Kathy admires most, visit the supplemental resources folder for this Hack. You may also follow Kathy on Instagram @kathrynzbrzezny.

Whether you're interested in learning more about structured notebook approaches or eager to see examples of whimsical, personalized notebooks, you'll find examples and notebook-keepers to connect to in the supplemental resources folder for this Hack. Use what you discover combined with your own understanding of what matters most inside of your workshop to create a vision for the notebooks that you and your students will create.

Consider reflecting on notebook use and your students' levels of satisfaction consistently throughout the year, to learn more about how you might improve the notebooking experience in your room.

It's easy to assume how writers are thinking and feeling, but I've learned that often, our assumptions are incorrect. Ask good questions of your notebook-keepers, and take their answers to heart. Let your students steer you toward improvement. This will help you elevate the quality of your students' notebooks while deepening your relationship with them. The support tools include:

- Slides that will help you and your students design and organize structured notebooks

- Photos of my charts and pages from Kathy Zbrzezny's notebook, as well as Hailey Barmasse's students' notebooks

- Conferring protocols that help writers leverage their notebooks as reflective tools

Image 5.3: Scan the code to find supplemental resources for supporting Hack 5.

CO-CREATE A JUST-RIGHT CURRICULUM

Designing agile frameworks that play well with others

If we eliminate the social factor from the child we are left only with an abstraction; if we eliminate the individual factor from society, we are left only with an inert and lifeless mass. Education, therefore, must begin with a psychological insight into the child's capacities, interests, and habits. It must be controlled at every point by reference to these same considerations. These powers, interests, and habits must be continually interpreted—we must know what they mean.
— JOHN DEWEY, PHILOSOPHER, PSYCHOLOGIST, AND EDUCATION REFORMER

THE PROBLEM: CURRICULUM OFTEN MISSES THE MARK

STANDARDIZED PROGRAMS AND curriculum maps initially appear to have several great advantages. First, they provide common, coherent, and comfortably linear pathways through learning experiences. They also emphasize outcomes, which helps teachers prioritize instruction and align their assessments accordingly. Programs and maps make for tight and efficient planning. They also intend to ensure equity. At least, I used to think so.

The problem with prefabricated programs and curriculum maps is that they're typically focused on the mastery of content and discrete skills rather than the study of learning. And what's engaging about that? Not much. Too many curriculum documents merely reference standards rather than achieving true alignment, and little attention is paid to the learner and the needs that emerge in real time. Curriculum writers often rely on weak evidence, outdated and even irrelevant data, and popular practices to predict what might work for students. They dedicate significant time to data entry as well, and this prevents them from studying learners and learning with real depth.

Finally, our tendency to accumulate frameworks of all shapes and sizes at every level of our systems creates a kind of noise that distracts us from deeper and more meaningful work. When the framework we use to design a writing curriculum doesn't play well with other frameworks, including mandated programs, we struggle to deliver on our promises to kids. Throw in all the frameworks we use to plan instruction, assessment, professional learning, teacher evaluation, program evaluation, data analysis, and more, and it's easy to understand why we keep saying change is hard. It certainly is, but perhaps it might be easier if we quit making things unnecessarily complex. In my experience, curriculum challenges often undermine our abilities to serve writers well.

THE HACK: CO-CREATE A JUST-RIGHT CURRICULUM

Emergent curriculum is responsive curriculum, and it can be the just-right curriculum for your students. It's evolving rather than prefabricated, and it ensures equity and the achievement of standards by putting the learner and the learning first. This type of curriculum is framed by teachers, but the details surface from the needs and interests of the writers in the room, and it is socially constructed. Teachers do not design emergent curriculum in isolation, ahead of meeting the writers they support. They design it beside them and in dialogue with them, as their shared learning unfolds.

IT TAKES TIME, PRACTICE, PROBLEM-SEEKING, AND SOLVING TO FULLY EMBRACE EMERGENT CURRICULUM DESIGN.

What might this look like?

In my experience, emergent curriculum is not directed or controlled by students, but rather, it emerges from the teacher-guided experiences they have in class. We create the context after crafting a shared vision for the learning and the way in which the learning will happen over the course of the year. We define the essential questions and the big ideas for each unit, and we also define the shared learning targets to meet. These decisions are not a result of mandated standards and test scores alone, but they are informed by immersing ourselves in our students' lives, observing them at work and play inside of it, and interviewing them about their experiences and the theories that emerge. The design process is driven by empathy.

EMPATHY DRIVES DESIGN THINKING

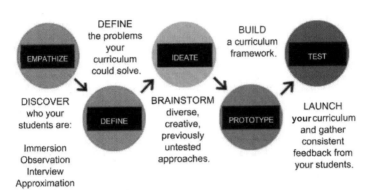

Image 6.1

As I explained in Hack 1, there are many ways to practice empathy inside of our writing workshops. Allowing the curriculum to emerge from learners' interests and needs expresses our commitment to a vision far greater than the curriculum itself: the creation of learning experiences that prepare all writers to be of influence in the world. Emergent curriculum is a vehicle for helping us achieve this vision because it brings writers' strengths to the surface so they can be recognized and leveraged. It engages learners in inquiry, problem-seeking, and problem-solving. It's collaborative, it inspires divergence, and it cultivates empathy and interdependence. It also provides writers the tools needed to become increasingly metacognitive, reflective, and discerning. These are the skills that writers in every field need.

Here's how you can begin: Try empathy mapping—a process by which writers explore and then reveal how their thoughts and feelings influence their interests, goals, and behaviors. When writers design empathy maps, I gain great insights about what matters most to them. For example, shortly after white supremacists clashed with counter-protesters in Charlottesville, Virginia, during the summer of 2017, I thought deeply about the difference that writing teachers could make in the lives of children who were living through such challenging times. I coached some to empathy map with their students, and this allowed them to think about what worried them most, what they were hearing, what they were seeing, what was influencing their thoughts and actions, and what their ultimate goals were as Americans who longed to make positive contributions to the conversations unfolding around them.

Through this work, we discovered that many young people were harboring a variety of unexpected fears and operating under assumptions that were wholly inaccurate. We also learned that most had theories about how peace could be achieved. More importantly, they knew how they might play a role in perpetuating it.

Rather than requiring students to write in responses to narrow prompts that were predetermined by teachers, empathy mapping inspired us to provide more options and divergent pathways through the process. This enabled students to pursue their specific interests about the topic and create diverse claims about a current event that confused them.

Writers also chose unique audiences for their pieces. They created rich and varied lines for inquiry, based on the learning targets that we previously set. Finally, as students immersed themselves in this work and we began moving our writing forward target by target, teachers kept up a daily dialogue with them about the discoveries they were making, their gains and pains as writers, and how the mini-lessons might better attend to their evolving interests and needs.

Teachers began with an understanding of what writers would produce, how they would produce it, and why—based on the findings from empathy mapping and learning targets aligned to the Common Core and other valued standards. The curriculum was negotiated with students day by day and one target at a time, as teachers leaned in, listened, and learned from their students' experiences. They didn't abandon the targets they prioritized at the outset of the unit, but rather, they refined and aligned them in ways that enabled students to pursue the standards, their interests, and their personal writing goals at the same time.

If you are interested in exploring curriculum frameworks and instructional practices that might guide a year, each unit, and each lesson in a similar manner inside of your own classroom, check out the supplemental resources folder for this Hack. It includes a variety of tools to help you design a just-right, emergent curriculum with the writers in your workshop or studio.

WHAT YOU CAN DO TOMORROW

Know that your initial efforts will be imperfect. It takes time, practice, and problem-seeking and solving to fully embrace emergent curriculum design. Set your own learning targets, document your learning, and share your stories along the way. Below are a few ways you can begin this journey right away.

- **EMPATHIZE.** Begin with what you know about the writers you serve. What are their strengths? What do they need? What interests them? What troubles them? Make curriculum choices based on what you know. Also, seek to understand whose stories are missing or incomplete, and what stories you need to hear in order to better understand your students. Peek at the supplemental resources folder for this hack. There, you'll find five empathy-building activities that will help you assess and monitor your students' interests and needs as they evolve over time.

- **DEFINE TARGETS AND INVITE INQUIRY.** Instructional objectives are written for teachers, and their purpose is to help teachers reach unifying outcomes. Learning targets are designed differently, and their purpose is to guide student learning. They describe what writers will come to know or be able to do within a single lesson, in language that they understand.

  Affinity mapping enables teachers to move, mix, and experiment with learning targets in ways that foster creative planning while still aligning to standards. This work is dynamic, engaging, and highly interactive. It challenges teachers to appreciate diverse perspectives and varied possibilities.

  If you haven't already, begin tomorrow by defining targets with students rather than doing this for them. For example, if the goal is to write a compelling letter to the editor of a local newspaper, invite students to analyze exemplars first. Challenge them to define the criteria that distinguish exemplars from non-exemplars. Then, invite them to create aligned learning targets rather than simply rolling out your local, state, or national standards. I'm not suggesting you evade them. I'm just recommending that you allow them to emerge from the study of quality exemplars first—because they often will. Add what's needed, but only after writers have the opportunity to inquire first.

Susan Brookhart and Connie Moss, authors of *Learning Targets: Helping Students Aim for Understanding in Today's Lesson,* remind us that targets don't have to be described in words for them to be effective. If photographs or demonstration videos make targets transparent for learners, all the better. The purpose of the target is to guide learning. Use the mediums and modalities that best accomplish this.

Once you have worked together to define learning targets and establish a coherent pathway through your unit, prepare to explore them with learners one at a time. As you introduce each new target, coach students to create lines of inquiry, word by word. Use what you learn about your students' interests and understandings to adjust remaining targets and invite deeper and perhaps divergent investigations. The supplemental resources folder for this hack includes stories, tools, and photographs that will support your efforts to apply these ideas in your own classroom.

- **PROTOTYPE AND ITERATE.**

In the future-ready workshop, teachers create contexts that elicit writers' interests in topics, skills, and ideas that they may not be aware of, let alone passionate about. They do this by immersing students in environments and presenting them with catalysts, materials, and constraints to draw out the desired learning, generate diverse perspectives, and even lead to conflicting narratives—rather than delivering single stories through narrow instruction.

To begin, try designing learning challenges and inquiries that align to established learning targets. Provide students with materials that create a bit of cognitive dissonance and ensure that the prompt, the materials, and the other constraints inspire divergent but purposeful thinking relative to the target.

For example, if I'm interested in helping writers establish a purposeful sequence for a narrative story, I might provide them with a box of wooden blocks and challenge them to build the sequence of their stories in just five minutes and then be ready to explain their reasoning. This catalyst aligns to our shared target, but the materials elevate the level of rigor and the potential for divergent work. Requiring students to explain their intentions makes this process more meaningful, too. Compare this to more traditional practices, where teachers define each part of a narrative and writers simply plug their ideas into their pre-cut frames.

Follow the QR code at the end of this Hack to explore other examples, strategies, and tools that will help you construct rich learning environments.

More important, treat your units and lessons—including those that live inside of prefabricated programs and maps—as prototypes. Remember, prototypes are low-res and low-risk. As you iterate and improve upon them, you'll assume the role of a designer who uncovers trouble and creates innovative alternatives rather than simply following prefabricated plans with blind fidelity.

- **CAPTURE WHAT MATTERS MOST.** Documentation is a powerful force inside of the emergent curriculum design process, especially when you inspire writers to make their learning visible, not just the products of it. Documenting this learning allows students to reflect on it, share it with others, and study it beside other artifacts that reveal important insights about their experiences, struggles, and growth.

Some encourage writers to capture as much of their process as possible, using diverse and even mixed mediums: photography, video, reflective journal writing, annotation, or audio recording. After writers have captured everything, they look into the data, searching for patterns and trends.

Others challenge writers to document their learning relevant to the agreed-upon target for the day, and they build time for documentation into the daily plan. It can be helpful to take a moment prior to beginning the day's work to orient writers to the documentation challenge. Pausing midway, and reflecting at the end, increases the likelihood that writers will be able to capture what matters most.

In my experience, when writers know the what, why, and how of documentation, the process proves far more meaningful. You'll find additional guidance and tools that support this work in the supplemental resources folder for this Hack.

- **EXTEND THE LEARNING THAT EMERGES.** Ask great questions, and listen to the answers that writers provide. Those who have taught in traditional workshops know the power of the writing conference. In recent years, I've fallen in love with targeted, over-the-shoulder conferences as well, and I'll say more about this in Hack 9.

  Co-designing a just-right, emergent curriculum with your students requires a different kind of dialogue, though: one that helps us notice, understand, and extend the unexpected learning that happens during inquiry and investigation.

  Whenever writers shift into exploration mode, it's important to position yourself both as a learner and their guide. This is where you will craft the learning experience. Your purpose and intention should always be to elevate the process and move the writers and their writing forward.

  You may have goals like these, and the prompts that follow can help you achieve them:

  - Recall what you already know about the writer, the work, and how to move both forward.

  - Assess the writer's strengths and needs and determine what is possible.

- Define exactly what you can build upon and grow, based on your investigation of the writer and the work.

- Create and sustain the writer's state of flow.

Before you open a dialogue with any writer, ask yourself, "What do I know?" Allow questions like these to guide your reflections, and know that it is common to realize that you do not yet have answers for all of them. Think about how might you get the answers. And if writers are unable to answer these questions for themselves, consider how their experiences with you might empower them to know themselves better over time.

Who is this writer?

What does this writer prefer to make, play, or do, beyond writing?

Which mediums does this writer prefer? Which modalities?

How much stamina does this writer have? How do I know when it's exhausted?

What is this writer's vision for his or her work?

In what ways does this writer hope to be an influence?

What knowledge does the writer have of this topic?

Which craft moves and process strategies has this writer already mastered?

What is this writer ready to learn?

What is this writer ready to try?

As you peek into the writer's work and process, ask yourself, "Where could this go?" Determine where the writer is inside of the inquiry process, in order to build bridges between divergent, emergent, and convergent thinking. Is the writer trying to generate an abundance of information, ideas, or possibilities? If so, questions like these are helpful:

What are some different ways to describe it?

What are all its parts?

How does it work?

How might you work it?

How many ways could you work it?

How many viewpoints can we consider from this?

What do you know?

What is unknown?

What should we investigate further?

Is the writer on the verge of making important connections between the information, ideas, and possibilities that emerged at the start of the inquiry work? Ask questions like these to expand these insights:

What are you seeing?

What's interesting here?

What's compelling you?

What patterns are emerging?

What themes do you notice?

What's speaking to you?

What seems important?

What connects?

What's missing?

What else should you investigate?

Is the writer weighing options, making determinations, evaluating, or prioritizing? These questions are useful:

What's best? Why?

What's most important? Why?

What's most meaningful? Why?

What's most useful? Why?

What would be most efficient? Why?

What's most beautiful? Why?

What's most interesting? Why?

What's most provocative? Why?

What's most inspiring? Why?

As you come to understand more about the writer's thinking and process, ask yourself, "What should I grow?" This extends the learning by asking questions that refine, challenge, or stretch the writer's thinking. Questions like these help:

What are you learning/writing/making? Have you considered this…?

Tell me everything you know about the part you're working on. What about this…?

What are you wondering? I'm wondering about this…

What are you confounded by? This is what's confusing me…

What do you want to know more about? Here's
what I'd like you to add…

How could you learn more about it? These
resources might be helpful…

How can I help you more?

**As writers sink deeper into their learning,
ask yourself, "What helps this writer flow?"**
When learners are in a state of flow, they are so
thoroughly engaged in their studies and work that
time has no meaning. Sometimes, flow is an enjoyable
and even peaceful state of being. Often, though, it
feels like tenacious problem-solving. Assessing writers'
states of flow will help you learn more about what
compels and focuses them and what does not. Ask
questions like these, and pay attention to how writers
respond. Don't force them down pathways on which
they aren't eager to travel. Uncover what inspires a
state of flow, and adjust your curriculum accordingly.

How are you feeling?

Which parts of this are really pulling you in?

What's the stone in your shoe, here?

What if you examined/tried/used this…?

How about…?

What should…?

Have you considered…?

What about…?

A BLUEPRINT FOR FULL IMPLEMENTATION

Step 1: Connect with experts; share with others.

Make an effort to connect with those who have greater expertise. In the supplemental resources folder for this Hack, I provide links to the thought leaders who have informed my work the most. Many of them are active on social media, blogging their own experiences, and eager to support you. Also, share your framework with administrators, teachers, support staff, students, parents, and community members. Explain how you use it, how others use it, and why it is of value. Most importantly, invite diverse interpretations and even a bit of tinkering. By now, you understand the essence of design thinking. It's that essence that matters, and sometimes, the mental models we create with good intentions diminish it. If your definition of design thinking is fixed, it's flawed.

Step 2: Empathize with each group of individuals in your system.

Learn more about their vision, strengths, and needs. Listen as they describe the challenges they face in their own work and the opportunities they're pursuing. Start paying even greater attention to how your system and each member in it functions. Consider how design thinking might enrich their work and their lives, and how it can help everyone support one another better. If others practice it differently than you do, what are the advantages?

Step 3: Define how you could help them use the framework to quiet their own noise and create alignment across the system.

Determine how you will share your experiences and expertise, and demonstrate the power of alignment. If everyone within your system developed a common (albeit nuanced) understanding of design, and if this framework drove learning in diverse contexts with diverse groups, which other frameworks could your system let go?

Step 4: Take full advantage of the framework's cyclical nature.

As you work through the process of co-designing learning experiences with your students, immersing them in inquiry, and allowing the curriculum to emerge, remember that this is a cyclical process rather than a linear one. It's also recursive in nature. Prototyping helps us understand more about who writers are, what they love, and what they need. We refine our targets in response. And as we prototype and play inside of our carefully constructed environments, it makes sense to share our own discoveries, our feelings, and the thinking behind the choices we make. This invites empathy all over again.

OVERCOMING PUSHBACK

Shifting away from prefabricated curricula and the programs that support them is liberating, motivating, and a bit frightening. Here are a few ways to overcome the most common challenges.

I don't have enough time to teach like this. Balance is key. Begin by identifying all the standards learners might attend to as they move through a learning experience. Then prioritize them. Which are must-dos and which are may-dos? Remember that when you shift to an inquiry-driven model, you elevate the rigor of the lesson or the unit. It's not uncommon for learners to pursue multiple targets at one time. Also, what they learn will be more likely to stick. Bloated programs don't guarantee the production of great writing or influential writers. Just because it looks complex on paper doesn't mean it will be in practice. Try selecting fewer standards and exploring them slowly, with far greater depth.

Our mandated program does not support emergent curriculum practices. Invite writers to investigate suggested modes of writing, essential questions, content, and skills inside of an emergent curriculum framework rather than a scripted one. Find ways to honor the alignment provided by the program while changing the environment and learning experiences. Look for places where can you flip a scripted, teacher-driven approach into an investigation- or inquiry-driven experience. I'll be honest: When systems adopt programs, I prefer that teachers implement them with fidelity first. They're prototypes. Test them and take copious notes. This will help you iterate based on what you know, rather than what you assume.

My students don't understand how to effectively communicate their interests, strengths, needs, or theories. This is common, particularly if writers haven't been asked to think and talk about this consistently in the past. We need to make space for this kind of learning in our workshops and studios. Define what this looks like, model it for them, and illuminate great examples when they unfold in front of you. There are a variety of protocols and tools that support writers through each phase of this process. Establishing clear expectations, procedures, and routines is important as well. Clarity and predictability help writers do more than merely function well inside of workshops. They embolden them to take risks. Take a peek at the supplemental resources folder for this Hack if you're seeking examples and tools that can help you more.

THE HACK IN ACTION

In Noelle Johnson's classroom at Roxborough Intermediate School in Littleton, Colorado, sixth-grade students begin co-designing their curriculum by deconstructing the central ideas for each unit they pursue and creating lines of inquiry that are personalized and meaningful to them. Recently, they unpacked the notion that expressing ideas leads to action. Students translated this statement word by word, teasing out the nuances and brainstorming diverse interpretations. Each artery on the mind map in Image 6.2 became a potential entry point for deeper investigation, experimentation, learning, and work.

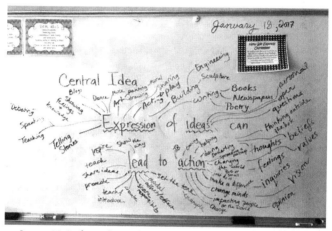

Image 6.2: Defining lines of inquiry within a shared learning target

Noelle expects her students to ideate and prototype through the process. Learners choose how they will engage with required content and how they will make their learning transparent. They also consistently assess their progress toward these goals. "This step needs to be guided by high-quality examples," she explained. "We analyze exemplars, and we also hold small group workshops to learn new technologies and support one another as we tinker with new content and skills." These meetings are led by students and teachers alike, and so are rounds of feedback. When students require a review, they call formal meetings or participate in what Noelle refers to as quick stand-ups: opportunities to share their successes and struggles, to grow the collective expertise of the group or engage in troubleshooting and problem-solving.

"We also test whether or not we are truly building knowledge, whether or not our learning is authentic, and whether or not it's meaningful and sustainable," Noelle continued. Her students define each of these ideas in class, using specific criteria and models. Then they revisit them often throughout the unit to monitor progress and make necessary adjustments.

Some might believe that Noelle's broadly themed International Baccalaureate units better enable her co-created curriculum, but this isn't necessarily the case. Inquiry supports any curriculum, if teachers are intentional about its use. If you would like to discuss her process, you'll find her on Twitter @NJohnsonROX.

When teachers get clear about what their curriculum must really control, they often realize it's far less than what they assumed. Defining unit outcomes, critical content, and discrete learning targets is important work, not only because it ensures alignment, but because it illuminates the white space in our frameworks, blueprints, and plans.

Invite your students to fill the white space. Plan how you will notice, note, and reflect on all that emerges as a result. The following tools, located in the supplemental resources folder below, may help you:

- Frameworks for emergent curriculum design
- Instructional practices that support this work

- Empathy-building activities

- A protocol for affinity mapping

- Stories and photographs that will bring the work of emergent curriculum design to life

Image 6.3: Scan the code to find supplemental resources for supporting Hack 6.

MAKE ROOM FOR SERIOUS PLAY

Discovering the power of loose parts

In any environment, both the degree of inventiveness and creativity, and the possibility of discovery, are directly proportional to the number and kind of variables in it.
— SIMON NICHOLSON, ARCHITECT AND TEACHER

THE PROBLEM: IMPENETRABLE TEXT

NEARLY FIFTY YEARS ago, Simon Nicholson postulated that when environments don't work—especially schools, playgrounds, daycare centers, art galleries, airports, and museums—it's because they don't meet what he refers to as the "requirement" of loose parts: materials that can be moved, mixed, ordered, combined, broken, remixed, and carried.

K'Nex are loose parts, and so are stones. Magnets are loose parts, and so are leaves. Springs are loose parts, and so are feathers.

Words are loose parts. Sentences are loose parts. Paragraphs and dialogue and lines of poetry: They are all loose parts. So, why do we pin them flat to static pages? Why do we require students to lock them down inside of graphic organizers? Why do we expect them to write draft by draft rather than iterating bit by bit?

Coherence matters in writing, but so does brilliance, and brilliance rarely emerges from first drafts or their revisions. Brilliance is the result of experimentation. Messing around. Tinkering. To achieve brilliance, writers need to get loose.

Given the right conditions—buttons and blocks, twigs and paper clips, and Play-Doh and Legos can elevate the writing process and the text that emerges from it. When we invite writers to use these mediums rather than print to generate, craft, and hone their ideas, they gain diverse perspectives. They think critically and creatively, too.

Let's challenge our writers to use loose parts like these to generate abundant ideas; discover, define, and expand the details in their writing; make a close study of their work; tinker; test; and play.

We can help writers treat text as a thoughtful arrangement of loose parts, too. They can break it, mix and remix it, and process their pieces bit by bit rather than draft by draft, to achieve brilliance.

Let's help our students *make* writing.

THE HACK: MAKE ROOM FOR SERIOUS PLAY

"Who are makers, anyway?" teachers ask whenever I speak to the connection between making and writing. Perhaps you are wondering, too. AnnMarie Thomas, author of *Making Makers*, reminds us that makers aren't certified. They self-identify. A maker is simply a person of any age who makes something. I used to assume that makers were strictly tech geeks like computer hackers and developers, but this definition is far too narrow.

Makers are artisans, hobbyists, and do-it-yourselfers who create all kinds of things using all kinds of materials. Some are scientists; others rehab classic cars. My husband has been brewing beer for well over a decade. He's a maker. I'm an avid gardener, and I love experimenting with different flower arrangements. I'm a maker that way, too. Makers often work in isolation, but more and more often they're finding company in makerspaces, workshops, studios, and other communities where they work on their projects and learn from one another. Many will tell you that they have O'Reilly Media and a guy named Dale Dougherty to thank for this.

In 2005, the Maker Movement began garnering the attention it enjoys today. This is when O'Reilly Media launched a magazine called *Make*. Each issue featured the work of different makers and showcased the interesting processes that they used. Readers were drawn to the people behind the projects, and every issue came dripping with do-it-yourself spirit and just enough direction to inspire people. As readership grew, so did the call for events that would bring them together.

Maker Faire founder Dale Dougherty extended the first invite in 2006, and the first Maker Faire was held in San Mateo, California. Three hundred makers and twenty-two thousand attendees came together to share ideas, demonstrate strategies, and test their prototypes. Seven years later, 120,000 people attended the Bay Area Maker Faire, and a hundred similar events were hosted worldwide. The rapid rise of the Maker Faire could be the result of Dougherty's commitment to one simple goal: Maker Faires exist to make more makers. Dougherty understood the power of network effects: When you connect ideas and people together, both grow.

This is how makers work: Rather than waiting on leaders to assign tasks, makers chase down formulas and examples themselves. They might follow the directions of others at first, but eventually, they begin hacking—redesigning processes or the tools they use to follow them. They try to create new forms and change the way things function. Nearly every maker I've studied used ideas, tools, and resources in ways they weren't originally intended.

ALL LEARNING IS KNOWLEDGE WORK, AND ALL TEACHERS AND WRITERS ARE DESIGNERS.

Makers also plan, design, perfect, and problem-solve bit by bit, tinkering with just one small element of the process or product they are creating and studying how small shifts in their approaches influence the outcome or the work.

This critical discovery inspired significant changes in my teaching practice. They're changes that I believe all writing teachers must make, because if we fail to do so, we will inadvertently silence scores of children who have important ideas to share and solutions to offer.

Writing is empowerment, but until we begin renovating our workshops and practices, many of our students will remain daunted by traditional definitions of writing, and unable or unwilling to engage in the methods we impose for producing it. The world is waiting for their contributions, and the web has made it easy for them to share. Our antiquated practices may very well be the only things inhibiting young writers now.

WHAT Y⊙U CAN DO TOMORROW

Creating a loose parts learning environment for writers isn't as daunting as it may seem. The steps below make for a quick start. Feel free to share your plans and questions on Twitter as you begin, using the #MakeWriting hashtag. I check the stream each day, and I'm happy to support you.

- **DISTINGUISH MAKING FROM ARTS AND CRAFTS.**
  Making isn't art, although art can be one way to make. It isn't necessarily intended to be appreciated for its beauty, or even for its emotional power. Making is also different from the sort of craft activities we often find inside of traditional classrooms. Making is about mixing, remixing, and repurposing loose parts to create something unique and, often, unexpected, that contributes to learning. Many makers will tell you that aesthetic isn't as important as the learning that emerges from the making experience or the way the product functions in the end. Prototypes, in particular, are often pretty ugly.

  When we make writing, we remove the barriers that print imposes on many writers. We remove the obligation to satisfy audiences with our art as well. Loose parts enable us to tell our stories, make our claims, and share our expertise without picking up a pen, powering up a device, or pursuing artistic perfection. Tinkering with loose parts helps us discover, clarify, expand, and refine our ideas. They evolve as we build, and our thinking does, too.

If we're going to work the relationship between making and writing to its fullest potential, we have to keep things loose. As Diane Kashin, co-author of *Empowering Pedagogy* explains, prefabricated kits and precut materials are the equivalent of fill-in-the-blank worksheets. They're chosen or designed by teachers, their use is directed by teachers, and what emerges is often redundant and the result of replication rather than creativity.

When we make writing, we use loose parts to create representations of our ideas. We work in metaphor and symbol. We let our hands take us where print cannot, and this is how we find our way back to it in the end. Are you eager to make your writing workshop a loose parts learning environment? You'll find inspiration in the supplemental resources folder for this Hack, including a tidy list of recommended loose parts.

Consider taking writers into new spaces, too. Get them outside; take them to a beach. Let them make and write inside of spaces where loose parts are found organically and ideas emerge from natural settings.

- **START A FIRE.** As we learned earlier, firestarters build background knowledge and ignite creativity ahead of your mini-lesson. These maker challenges include a variety of constraints: time, materials, and a powerful prompt that is aligned to the day's learning target. You'll find a set of firestarter ideas in the supplemental resources folder for Hack 2, but you can use the formula shown in Image 7.1 to design your own.

Firestarters are:

Catalysts for critical thinking.
Challenges that ignite inquiry.
Tools for scaling print barriers.

The Formula:

Given X resources
and
X amount of time
How might you...?

Quality Creations Are:

Illuminating, Tangible,
Clearly Justified

Image 7.1: The firestarter formula

- **LET THEM BREAK STUFF.** A break-it box is a container full of stuff that kids can rip apart and repurpose. It's a great alternative to the garbage bin, extending the life and elevating the purpose of discarded appliances, devices, and other products. Invite donations, and encourage kids to tear into whatever they find in the box. Tell them not to think about what the item is. Inspire them to think about what it could be. Let them mess around with the guts that live inside of the items they find there. This is how they will learn about how things work. They'll find inspiration for their stories, arguments, and explainer texts there, too.

Encourage them to treat the work of writers they admire in the same way. How might they break their work into loose parts? How can they mix diverse mentor texts, remix them, or synthesize loose parts from both? What can they learn from this kind of dissection and intersection? What could be created in the process?

- **ENCOURAGE SWITCHING**. Print is just one modality, and many argue that it isn't even the modality of the moment. Future-ready writers know how to use diverse mediums and modalities to inform, move, and call their readers to action. Does your writing workshop prepare them for this reality? I began inviting writers to switch mediums or modalities whenever they told me they were blocked. "Build what you don't yet have words for," I suggested. "Sketch it. Paint it. Perform it. Dance out the conflict in your story." Every time, words began to flow in the wake of making. When I encourage print-confident kids to translate their manuscripts into new mediums or modalities, they're often uncomfortable at first.

They're perfectionists, some of them. They don't like being novices, and making makes beginners of us all. It's important to make space for this and to expect it. If we're going to help print-confident writers be of real influence in this world, it's important that we help them sharpen other skills that matter.

- **GAMESTORM.** Dave Gray, Sunni Brown, and James Macanufo, co-authors of *Gamestorming: A Playbook for Innovators, Rulebreakers, and Changemakers* challenge their readers, largely comprised of business leaders, designers, and developers, to distinguish the pursuit of incremental improvement from that of creativity. This is a crucial consideration for those striving to build the world's most innovative organizations.

  They suggest that managing for incremental improvement motivates the use of reliable, repeatable, and consistent processes that lead to predictable results (much like traditional workshop structures do). Managing for creativity emboldens those we lead to create very differently, and what's produced is often remarkable, distinctive, and delightful.

  All learning is knowledge work, and all teachers and writers are designers. Many traditional writing workshop structures enable us to manage for incremental improvement. While many long for a more creative, free-range experience, they're uncertain how to achieve it without creating complete disorder, undermining productivity, and compromising quality.

  Traditional writing workshop lessons motivate

teachers to create secure chains of instruction. Gamestorming transforms the model, engaging writers directly with frameworks and processes that spur rapid ideation, opportunities for collaborative exploration and experimentation, and far superior decision-making. Writers still pursue clear outcomes, and the sequence of their learning is coherent, but this is writing off the chain. This is how writers manage for creativity while pursuing incremental improvement.

I appreciate this need to manage for creativity— it's why I recommend gamestorming. So what's in a game? It includes much of what you'd expect: a clear objective, a set of rules, tight boundaries, a board, and pieces to manipulate. Players have one goal, but everyone can win.

Students play a game in three acts. A set of deceptively simple game boards—typically whiteboards, windows, walls, charts, or tables—enable this work, allowing writers to lead their own learning and make it visible while providing teachers more time to study it from the sidelines.

The opening act of every game is distinguished by a set of firestarters: powerful questions and rapid prompts that spark a blaze of diverse ideas. This is divergent thinking. During the second act, writers engage in collaborative and highly disciplined experimentation. Ideas are randomized, organized, mixed, and remixed. Patterns surface. Synthesis occurs. This is emergent thinking. The third act is all about closure: Writers establish priorities, make decisions, and are released back into the workshop prepared to begin new projects or iterate on the old. This is divergent thinking. If you're interested in learning more, drop into the supplemental resources folder for this Hack. There you'll find a wide variety of games, photos, and stories from the road, in addition to links to the Gamestorming website, which is packed with additional protocols for use with different groups in varied settings.

A BLUEPRINT FOR FULL IMPLEMENTATION

Once writers have established a taste for loose parts play and you've had the opportunity to experience the difference between traditional teaching and controlling for creativity, you might begin wondering how to position yourself more often as a facilitator rather than a director. These are big steps, but they'll get you there.

Step 1: Coach creative theft.

In his bestselling book, *Steal Like an Artist*, Austin Kleon validates everything I've ever said to parents and teachers who worry when kids begin writing fan fiction.

"My daughter just ripped off J.K. Rowling," a concerned mother will tell me, and I'll find myself pulling on some version of Kleon's words in response. Nothing is original, he reminds us. Everything is a remix. "Stealing is okay," I'll reassure her.

But … *stealing isn't simple.* I find that kids need to be taught how to steal with integrity. After all, there's a big difference between mixing and remixing ideas until distinctively different work emerges, and simply tacking a few of our ideas on top of someone's original work and calling the result our own.

When adults who know better do this, it's called plagiarism. When young writers do this, savvy teachers try to treat it as a developmental phase. Then, they make it their responsibility to teach their students how to steal with integrity. Explicitly.

Image 7.2 provides a peek into the process, as I often demonstrate it for my students. You'll find links to lessons and my favorite tools and strategies for coaching creative theft in the supplemental resources folder for this Hack. I've included links to Austin Kleon's books, blogs, and videos there as well.

Image 7.2: Coaching creative theft

Step 2: Use protocols.

As I explained in Hack 6, teachers might define the forms and the learning targets that writers pursue in each unit of study, but the writers blaze their own trails through them. We may guide writers down purposeful paths, but as Brian Kissel, author of *When*

Writers Drive the Workshop explains, its writers who determine the detours.

Gamestorming gives us a frame for making this journey as creative and productive as possible, and there are other protocols that serve our quest to become facilitators rather than directors of learning. They enable writers to generate their own ideas, investigate forms and the work of other writers independently, move through their own processes, self-assess, and improve their own work. Most importantly, these protocols establish a level of equity that cultivates interdependence and enables writers to turn toward one another for guidance and support, rather than over-relying on the teacher.

Step 3: Ask better questions and make time for reflection.

"Lean in and listen hard," I suggest whenever teachers tell me they're uncertain how to serve writers best. This is how we get to know who our students are, what they love, and what they need. Experience has taught me that if I'm hoping to learn anything meaningful, I need to ask savvy and strategic questions. This realization transformed the way I assess, confer, and provide feedback. It elevates learning during loose parts play, too. Here are five different ways loose parts play moves writers and their writing forward, and the questions I ask that inspire the connection. You'll find others in the supplemental resources folder for this Hack.

Making helps writers generate ideas. Ask:

> What did making help you discover about your topic, stance, or story?
>
> How will these discoveries shape your writing?

Making helps writers define the whole of their topics as well as the parts. Ask:

> How does your build help you define your topic?
>
> How does your build help you define the next part? All parts?

Making helps writers tease out details. Ask:

> Which details might enhance your build even further?
>
> How will the details in your build elevate your draft?

Making helps writers zoom in on what's most important. Ask:

> What do you notice about each part when you break your build into bits?
>
> How might you use these details to craft your writing?

Making inspires new ideas, encouraging writers to deviate from their original ideas and plans. Ask:

> How did making change your thinking?
>
> How will it change your writing?

Step 4: Coach them to document their learning.

Documentation helps makers and writers understand and share their learning stories. The data captured through the documentation process—such as photos, videos, and writing samples—serve as the loose parts of a far greater narrative.

When writers mix and remix those parts, they often draw new conclusions, and different perspectives about their learning and work emerge. When they make their learning visible, the stories they tell themselves about their writing and their work evolve. These narratives serve the writer, the teacher, and even greater audiences who hope to learn more from the writer's experiences. This is a powerful impetus that transitions writers to print.

I realized this during the summer of 2017 when Chappaqua Central School teacher Kathy Rowland made a point of photographing a young writer as he built and rebuilt a tower in a Make Writing pop-up studio that I was leading. Kathy was a teacher participant who was particularly sensitive to the needs and interests of the more resistant writers in the room.

I wasn't surprised when she asked this young man if she could photograph his build in progress. I was impressed when his eyes lit up as she showed him the images later, and I was warmed by the understanding that the two of them seemed to share. He realized that he could use the photos in a bunch of different ways. Maybe he would write a fictional story that featured the tower. Maybe he would write about his experiences as a builder. Maybe he'd share the intention behind his design.

The possibilities were endless, and the exchange taught me something important: When writers engage in documentation and reflection, they're doing more than examining their learning. They're discussing it; opening it to interpretation; turning it over in their minds; and reconciling it with their hearts. They're finding themselves in the stories that emerge, and they're also curating ideas for future writing pieces.

Step 5: Join them.

When teachers position themselves as writers and makers in the workshops and studios they facilitate, the energy in the space shifts dramatically. Rather than viewing you as an expert and an evaluator, your students will come to know you as a learner. Share your curiosities with them. Share your joy, and your struggles, too. Show them how you muddle through. Join them in their loose parts play. Make some writing of your own. I know very few writing teachers who identify as writers themselves, but your students will make you one if you let them support you as much as you support them.

OVERCOMING PUSHBACK

The notion of making for the purposes of writing is fairly uncommon in traditional writing workshop circles, so whenever I work with veteran writing teachers on the ground, I'm accustomed to answering quite a few questions and helping people wrestle with a bit of dissonance. These are my responses to the issues that seem to challenge people the most.

My budget is tight. This is the beauty of loose parts play: It isn't necessary to spend a fortune to begin making. Use what you have on hand, for starters. Rifle through your junk drawers, dip into the recycling bin, and dig out any materials and supplies left over from other projects. Turn to nature for inspiration as well. Invite students to build with sticks, stones, leaves, and flower heads. Teach them to respect and protect living things, but show them how loose parts live in our natural environment. Finally, ask parents and students for donations, particularly around the holidays. Packing peanuts, boxes, and Styrofoam parts are valuable resources inside of a makerspace.

I don't have anywhere to store all this stuff. Much of the making that writers do in workshop is low-resolution prototyping. They build to clarify, expand, refine, and share their thinking. The materials are cheap, time is limited, and the commitment to the aesthetic is very light. Let your students know that they have two choices once the builds are complete: They can take them apart or they can take them home. Photos preserve the memory of builds that matter most, but none of the builds need to be saved. The loose parts you gather don't need to take up a ton of space, either. While some teachers love to keep a stackable set of tinker trays on hand and others fashion mobile makerspaces out of supply or tech carts, there are teachers who provide kids limited materials and place tight boundaries around how they use them. They realize that these constraints inspire creativity. They know that the real makerspace isn't in the room; it's in the minds and hands of the writers who work there.

What if they fall in love with building and still refuse to write?
Author Anne Lamott is celebrated for her theory of the one-inch picture frame. She tells writers that no matter how overwhelmed, uninspired, or intimidated she is by the thought of writing, it helps to demand nothing more from herself than a description that can fit inside of a one-inch picture frame. A sticky note is two by two, and I find those parameters just as powerful.

When we ask students to build bit by bit, it's easier to transition them to print. Don't ask them to map the whole story. Invite them to build just the main character. They might label each detail when they're finished, and those words will shape their written descriptions. Don't expect them to put down an entire draft, either. Remember the theory of the one-inch picture frame. Rather than handing them an 8.5x11 sheet, start with a two-by-two sticky note. If you demand nothing more at once, you'll rarely get anything less. It's easier to get traction with your most resistant writers this way.

Something else: If what they're building might engage audiences more than print, consider the fact that the product might be meeting a far greater purpose. Writing doesn't often look like print out in the wild. Don't miss the forest for the trees.

THE HACK IN ACTION

When elementary teachers from Buffalo, New York, began inviting students to use loose parts in their writing workshops, the results were more than encouraging. "They all have ideas," said Omarlla Roulhac, Director of Instruction and Curriculum. "Even the kids who claim to hate writing are able to plan really interesting pieces when they use loose parts."

Teachers can assess with precision as well. As writers make things they may not have words for, it's easier to define where print barriers are getting in the way and what writers have the capability of saying once the barriers are removed. When the New York State Department of Education mandated the use of pre- and post-assessments for teacher evaluation purposes, teachers worried about the potential for over-testing, and especially, the potential hit to engagement and confidence levels. Rather than disrupting learning to evaluate it, they invited kids to use loose parts to show what they knew about the structure of informational texts and their capacities to gather facts from research. You'll find this case study and supporting photographs in the supplemental resources folder for this Hack.

"So many kids love to work with different mediums," primary level teacher Katie Greene revealed. "Their confidence soars whenever we let them use art materials to express themselves. This showed up in our assessments, and they loved working this way. It didn't feel like a test. They didn't know they were being tested."

Adults often respond the same way, and this raises an interesting question: How might defining oneself as a writing teacher make the act of writing more daunting for teachers? Heather McKay is a literacy specialist for the Calgary Board of Education in Alberta, Canada. As a professional learning facilitator, she supports many teachers, who by their own admission, struggle to find the time and confidence required to define themselves as writers. "Although whenever I use manipulatives, teachers are more willing to play," she told me.

Heather invites teachers to treat the texts that they value most, and the ones that they produce, as loose parts. They study pieces bit by bit, write with sticky notes and index cards, and as much as possible, make writing a physical endeavor.

She coaches them to practice creative theft as well. "When teachers have strong examples of what they're eager to create in front of them, and when they have permission to mix and remix parts of other teachers' work, they become more playful," she explained. "This produces stronger writing and more creative results."

It's a more equitable process that inspires greater ownership, too. When teachers realize that writing can involve loose parts play—generating ideas, tinkering around with them, writing, revising, and moving things around—they begin to view writing as an active process that they can claim as their own rather than the completion of a task that has been imposed on them.

"This helps teachers create their own writing identities," she concluded. "We're taking ourselves and the task a bit less seriously, realizing that we don't have to immediately write 'right,' and focusing more on the process rather than the product."

Heather explained that the teachers she supports often create heartfelt works. "I get to know them better through their work. Some of it is so funny, too." And when those teachers have the courage to share their pieces with their peers, "their smiles grow," Heather told me. "It feels good when people appreciate you as a writer."

While many writers who build and break and write with loose parts tell me that the shift is transformational, sometimes it's not so much. At least once a week, I'm given pause by examples of loose parts play that people share with me by email or in my social networks. Sometimes, kids don't move beyond building, and what they're building lacks complexity. Sometimes, it lacks any real meaning at all.

It's easy to throw a bunch of Legos at kids and tell them to make something, but if the experience doesn't move writers and their writing forward, there is little return on a great investment of time, which is precious inside of the writing workshop. When making elevates writing, it adds to the learning. When making replaces writing or allows resistant writers to evade it altogether, we need to re-evaluate our practices. If you are grappling with these issues, you may find the next Hack particularly helpful. Before you go, take a peek at the supplemental resources for this Hack, though. They include:

- A list of loose parts that won't break the bank

- Approaches for coaching creative theft

- Gamestorming routines and links to the giants whose shoulders I stand on: Dave Gray, Sunni Brown, and James Macanufo

- Additional protocols that empower a writer-centered workshop

Image 7.3: Scan the code to
find supplemental resources
for supporting Hack 7.

HACK 8
TINKER THROUGH THE PROCESS
Finding new ways to draft and revise bit by bit

The maker movement leads to a new pedagogy—
Tinkquiry—Tinkering + Inquiry.
— PETER SKILLEN, MICROSOFT GLOBAL HERO IN EDUCATION

THE PROBLEM: PRINT RESISTANCE

IT TOOK A long time for me to recognize my arrogance. Like many teachers, I thought what I did with my markers and chart paper and chalk was important. I thought I was deserving of respect every time I assumed my teacher stance at the front of the room, and I was largely intolerant of students who didn't provide it.

I thought I was the master. The sage that my students needed—even wanted—on the stage.

Decades later, I now know that students are wiser than many give them credit for, and if we let them, they often become our greatest teachers.

Once they leave our buildings at the end of each day, many "struggling students" aren't defined by their resistance to writing or their failure to succeed in a thousand other ways at school. They're artists, musicians, engineers, and electricians. They're teaching themselves HTML and sewing costumes and baking cakes and starting garage bands. I remember how, during my first year of teaching, several of my most challenging students told me about the forts they built in the woods out of scrap bits of lumber and other materials they salvaged (okay, they might have stolen them) from neighborhood garages. I told them that I built forts like these with my friend, Chrissy, way back in the 1980s. They liked me more in that moment, and I gained a newfound respect for them, too.

Here's the thing: Writing and making are human endeavors that stand the test of time. They connect us. They help us know ourselves and one another better. Genuine learning is the same across humankind.

The resistant writers I've worked with over the last two decades were the ones who helped me realize that making is a gateway to writing. Whenever I invite kids to make in any capacity inside of writing workshops, they're far more willing to put down words.

I never spoke about "making writing" when I began noticing the connection between these two endeavors early in my career. I didn't reap the greatest rewards of this discovery until I left the comfortable bubble of my own classroom. As a professional learning service provider, I've spent over a decade working full time beside teachers in very different kinds of schools as they've supported very different kinds of writers.

Together, we watched reluctant writers find their very first words inside of the things that they built. We realized that making helped many dedicated writers conceptualize the parts of their drafts that they were struggling to compose. Each of these experiences confirmed the observations I made long ago: Making was engaging, it inspired abundant ideas, and it elevated the quality of drafts in progress, particularly when writers made things that helped them meet writing-related targets.

There was just one problem: Too many students were unwilling to sit still long enough to complete detailed drafts. They struggled to stay silent. They were eager to keep moving and building and experimenting and playing. They wanted to mess around with the projects they were working on at home, and no amount of sitting in a desk and tinkering with writing tasks satisfied them.

Nothing about our writing experiences enabled the sort of self-motivated and directed learning they were experiencing on their own. In fact, the invitation to make in class inspired some students to evade the writing experience altogether. This was the stone in my shoe. If you've been struggling to integrate making and writing, I'll bet that you know this pain.

Perhaps you're familiar with a few of these other common challenges, too:

- The Fast Finish: The distance between beginning and completing the draft is measured in mere minutes.

- One and Done: If revisions are attempted, they're made at the surface level.

- The Short and Shallow Draft: These pieces often lack development. Stories tell, rather than show. Information and argument writing attends to basic facts but lacks detail.

- The Long List: Stories read like a list of action statements. Characters move through a series of events rapidly, and the writer fails to include important context, such as how those characters think or feel. Information and argument writing includes an overabundance of facts, listed in quick, often incoherent order.

- The Neverending Story: Here, writers sink so deeply into the internal world they've created, or their own interests as researchers, that they fail to find and write with a meaningful purpose that readers will appreciate.

Similarly, you might find yourself confronting a workshop full of writers who claim to be "done" while other writers have not yet begun. Some might treat graphic organizers like fill-in-the-blank worksheets. Others might refuse to plan altogether. And once those drafts are complete? You find yourself struggling to produce the right amount and kind of feedback. When writers fail to respond to feedback productively, you find yourself admitting defeat.

Does any of this sound familiar? Congratulations! You've earned your writing teacher stripes. You're also ready to become a design thinker.

THE HACK: TINKER THROUGH THE PROCESS

Design thinkers ground the things they make in the experiences of their users. As I explained earlier, empathy drives design. In this way, your most resistant writers can become your most valuable teachers. Ask them why they struggle to put down print. Lean in and listen hard to their answers. Shift your practice in ways that meet their needs without diminishing your own. Control for quality, but ask: How might we write in ways that move these writers forward? Your solutions will likely be different from mine because your students are not my students. Regardless of this reality, I've found that prototyping prior to drafting, and tinkering through the process, often helps.

You might recall my description of pro- **THINK OF EACH**
totypes in the introduction. They're a low- **FORM OF WRITING**
risk and low-commitment endeavor. They're **AS A BUILD,**
made with inexpensive materials, and
they're meant to be fiddled with, bit by bit. **CONSTRUCTED**
When we prototype, we intend to fail fast **FROM BLOCKS**
in order to move forward. Loose parts play **OR BITS.**
often involves prototyping, but it's no substitution for print, and in the writing workshop, print still matters. So when I discovered that many of my most resistant writers self-defined as makers, I found myself confronting this question: How might we make writing?

One solution: breaking the whole of any piece into loose parts and processing around each piece. Rather than moving writers through the process as they complete an entire unit, help them work the process around each bit, over and over again. If you need clarity, the steps that follow might help you, and you'll find additional resources that support each one in the supplemental resources folder for this Hack.

WHAT YOU CAN DO TOMORROW

Start small, perhaps with just one unit. Take each step below, as you help students tinker through the process. Feel free to reach out to me on Twitter to share your experiences, troubleshoot, and problem-solve. You'll find me in the #MakeWriting stream @AngelaStockman.

- **ANALYZE AND DEFINE THE BLOCKS.** Think of each form of writing as a build, constructed from blocks or bits. You'll find simple examples for narrative, information, and argument writing in image 8.1. These are merely illustrative. It makes sense to help writers define their own blocks using examples provided by authors they admire. Many call these mentor texts, and when we investigate them with purpose, writers learn that great writing involves inquiry.

BUILD EACH FORM BIT BY BIT.

Narrative Writing				
SOMEBODY	WANTED	BUT	SO	THEN

Opinion/Argument Writing				
OPINION	REASON	REASON	REASON	CALL TO ACTION

Information Writing				
TOPIC	FACT	FACT	FACT	CLOSING

Figure 8.1: Blocking three common forms of writing

- **MAKE TIME FOR IDEATION.** This was my first realization as a new teacher of writing who wanted to do better: The quality of the final product rises and falls in relation to the quality of each writer's brain-storming experience. Rather than positioning brain-storming as the first phase in "the" process, coach writers to brainstorm again and again, as they revisit the process inside of each bit. Kids need to ideate as they approach each block of a form, not simply at the beginning, to generate topics or the general structure for each piece. If you're uncertain how to proceed, you'll find inspiration and ideas worth replicating in the supplemental resources folder for this Hack.

Process Each Bit.

Image 8.2: Processing around a single bit

- **LET THEM MAKE.** The beauty of prototyping bit by bit is that writers may make if they'd rather not print. Invite them to build their main characters, their claims, or the central ideas of the pieces that inform. The challenge is to make only a single bit of the whole. No more, and certainly no less. When they're finished, invite them to analyze their build, listing words for each detail they notice. Then, invite them to use the words to write just that tiny bit of their drafts.

Give each one an index card. Remind them of Anne Lamott's one-inch picture frame. Let them drop a bit of text onto a two-by-two sticky note. Just one block, not the whole. This is how we write bit by bit.

- **TINKER, TEST, AND ITERATE**. Don't let them rush ahead. Writing bit by bit allows us to provide tightly targeted and perfectly differentiated feedback. Experienced writers and those who are passionate about print may stretch that two-inch sticky note into a longer bit of text, but it's not the length that matters—it's what they're doing with all that print.

Assess their work by peering over their shoulders, identify what they're doing well, and feed them forward with just-right suggestions. Expect each one of them—including your strongest and most print-confident writers—to tinker hard with each small bit of writing. Rather than inviting them to move ahead, inspire them to revise each bit multiple times, trying different approaches, and even testing them on potential readers. Coach your students to take the feedback seriously, but not to heart. Remind them that these are prototypes. We need to fail fast and try again, to reach our fullest potential.

Move toward the next block only when you're certain that every writer has brainstormed, drafted, tinkered, tested, and revised the text relevant to the current block. Teach your fastest and most impatient writers to make their texts increasingly complex rather than rushing ahead. Encourage them to write deeper inside the current block rather than moving forward.

A BLUEPRINT FOR FULL IMPLEMENTATION

In my experience, when teachers align the tinkering instructional practice with their curriculum planning and assessment practices, the quantity and quality of student writing improves. This is important work that takes time and a bit of trial and error. Here's how you can begin:

Step 1: Define the learning targets and lessons that live within each block.

What will writers need to investigate and demonstrate their learning to masterfully craft each block of the form? When we're clear about what matters, we're better able to define the mini-lessons, the invitations into inquiry, and the depth of learning we're expecting writers to achieve. This helps us understand what all learners must know and be able to do, and what some might learn and do, depending on their interests and needs.

Step 2: Differentiate instruction.

Differentiating instruction helps students write deeply into a block rather than rushing forward without realizing their full potential. It also enables less experienced writers to produce quality work within each block without reaching unproductive levels of frustration. Consider differentiating your targets and anchor charts as you share them with writers. You'll find examples in the supplemental resources folder for this hack.

Step 3: Feed writers forward in just-right ways.

Anticipate the areas where writers will be successful, where they will struggle, and what you will see in their work, relevant to each target. Then think about the different kinds of feedback you will offer to different writers. Consider how you might move them forward in just-right ways by helping them tinker through the process. You'll find feedback frames aligned to specific targets and differentiated for writers of different experience levels in the supplemental resources folder for this Hack.

Step 4: Scaffold them toward new and more complex forms.

As writers master simple forms, invite them to investigate others that are more complex. Ask them to define the additional blocks in these new forms and determine how writers developed them. Challenge them to add these new blocks to their own prototypes. Support this experimental work and remember, their willingness to try new and more difficult things should be assessed, but not evaluated. It reveals a lot about their progress toward higher level learning targets. Elevate their strengths, and help them frame their struggles positively and productively.

While your efforts to help students write bit by bit may attend to more traditional forms that all writers in your workshop must master, it's important to help students learn how to block any form they hope to experiment with. This is a lifelong writing skill that will empower them to live like writers long after they leave your space.

OVERCOMING PUSHBACK

Tinkering through the writing process is a new concept for many educators, students, and their families, and anything that's new invites pushback. Here are my responses to common concerns:

Some of my students don't want to write this way. That's okay. It's common for some writers to prefer paper and screen to sticky notes and index cards, and when I encounter writers like this, I'm careful not to choose their tools. However, the other practices that

I'm recommending in this Hack are essential components of quality curriculum design, instruction, and assessment. Writers need to know their learning targets, they need to write deeply rather than quickly crafting the surface of each block, and they need to develop and experiment with approaches that help them master and move beyond these targets. We must help them meet these goals by providing just-right feedback. Most students find it far more efficient and rewarding to write bit by bit using movable and mixable tools to achieve these goals, but others should be welcome to use traditional tools if they prefer, if this doesn't impede their progress.

It's important for kids to write long. Volume matters, which is why it's not enough to simply invite making in our workshops. Ironically, this is also why writing bit by bit rather than draft by draft matters, too. A bit is a manageable amount of text for writers to produce, assess, tinker with, and stretch. This approach isn't about limiting the amount of print that writers put down. It's about scaffolding writers with precision, enabling them to strive for sophistication, and increasing the complexity of their learning, and ultimately, their work. It's important to move writers through the writing process as they attend to each bit, and show them how to stretch into each one. One and done is not an option here. Experimentation, tinkering, and revision are required. Show them how constraints can help them produce more and better writing.

Blocking the form and building bit by bit takes more time, and I don't have it. It does. However, it leads to a considerable return on the time investment. When we block forms and process around each block, writers improve the quality of their work bit by bit throughout the experience. This results in higher-quality drafts that require less revision and editing. It also decreases your paper load and frustration. When we wait until drafts are completed to provide robust feedback, both the teacher and the writer can feel overwhelmed by the enormity of issues. Take it one bit at a time, provide a small amount of feedback on a small amount of text, and watch how they dive into the work of revision. They'll experiment more within each block as well.

THE HACK IN ACTION

Before second-grade teacher Krista Jensen began writing bit by bit with her students, she noticed their low stamina for writing. An experienced teacher from Calgary, Alberta, Canada, she was disheartened by the lack of enthusiasm she witnessed in her Battalion Park School students. "At least one-third of my students disliked writing and a handful were completely resistant," she revealed. "Most would attempt to do what was required of them as writers, but their work looked much like the models I shared, and there was very little revision happening at all." Krista noticed that most of the changes that writers were willing to make focused on errors in conventions only, and she knew that editing and revision were very different animals.

After she introduced tinkering concepts, her students' writing stamina increased immediately. "This is what made writing with sticky notes fabulous," she said. "Using small pieces of paper was less overwhelming. It was easier for writers to add ideas and change them around without having to start all over."

When writers use sticky notes, nothing is ever lost to the revision process. They might sideline ideas, but the notes make it easy to call them back into play or move them elsewhere when needed. "My students' willingness to revise and edit increased as they gained a clearer understanding of how each form was structured and how they could play with each bit."

Krista learned that constraints were important, too. She color-coded the sticky notes to help writers distinguish the blocks from one another, limited the tools she provided, and ensured that writers tinkered around a tight target. "Too much choice was stifling," she explained. "Most students need support and clear guidelines to ensure the move from play to print."

Gamestorming helps Krista's students write deeply into each block. They play a game called Storyboard That! to generate and tinker with narrative writing elements, and another, called Emoji Mapping, pushes new writers to consider the thoughts and feelings of the characters they create. Float Your Question helps Krista ensure total participation in the inquiry process that frames the beginning of her information writing unit, and loose parts play winds its way through the entire year. You'll find games like these and many more in the supplemental resources folder for this Hack, along with lesson plans and peeks into other classrooms where teachers and writers are learning how to tinker through the process bit by bit.

Michelle Shelton is reaping the rewards of writing bit by bit with the writers in her freshman English class at Oxford High School in Oxford, Alabama. I connected with Michelle when she interviewed me for her podcast, *Across the Hall*, which she co-hosts with Cade Somers.

"Most of my students feel very inadequate as writers," she told me. "They do not enjoy writing and they've said that they don't think they're good at it. They have a difficult time understanding what a prompt requires of them, and they don't dig very deeply into analysis, either. They often just skim the surface. When they're given any kind of freedom to write what they want to write, they shut down."

Michelle invited writers to make writing for the first time in the fall of 2017, as her students began blogging. "I modeled for them.

I showed them examples of various blog posts. I included introduction activities and discussion in the lesson leading up to the writing," she explained. "And their posts still ended up being about a paragraph in length with little organization or visual appeal."

She worked backwards, using her own completed blog post to model how a writer might break that whole form into loose parts. "I cut paper into pieces that were about half the size of an index card, and I gave them each eight pieces to start," she said. "I showed them how I used one card for the title, one for each image that I wanted to include in my post, and one for each subheading. Then, I showed them how I might play around with the order to make it look the way I wanted it to look and to make sure the information was ordered logically and had the effect I desired."

This approach had solid results. "The students were engaged!" Michelle said. "They drew pictures on their cards and pulled out quotes that they could use. They played around to come up with the best possible titles and made sure they had plenty of information to fill the space they wanted to fill."

Michelle witnessed firsthand the connection to making. "They were actually building their blog posts. When they transferred the posts from the cards to the blog itself, they learned about how to incorporate images in a way that was more visually appealing and how to use font to highlight important points. It was amazing, the transformation that occurred."

If you are eager to see photos of Michelle's process, her students at work, and links to their before-and-after posts, just dive into the supplemental resources folder for this Hack. You'll be able to connect with Krista there, too.

Blocking each writing form, defining clear learning targets, and offering writers just-right feedback enables us to do more than engage, empower, and attend to the needs and interests of the different writers we support. It makes for more timely and productive assessment as well. See what's waiting for you in the supplemental resources folder below:

- Strategies for generating ideas with students

- Examples of differentiated charts

- Feedback frames that will help you and your students talk with one another in targeted and supportive ways

- Stories and photos from Michelle Shelton's and Krista Jensen's classrooms

Image 8.3: Scan the code to find supplemental resources for supporting Hack 8.

HACK 9

UNCOVER AND SHARE LEARNING STORIES

Documenting evidence of learning

Stand aside for a while and leave room for learning, observe carefully what children do, and then, if you have understood well, perhaps teaching will be different from before.
— LORIS MALAGUZZI, FOUNDER OF THE REGGIO EMILIA EDUCATIONAL PHILOSOPHY

THE PROBLEM: MOST ASSESSMENTS DON'T CLOSE THE LOOP

SCHOOLS HAVE BECOME increasingly skilled at gathering data about learners—particularly quantitative data in the form of standardized and local test scores. These data perpetuate many theories about performance, but they often fail to communicate the most essential information that teachers need in order to serve students well. They might help us develop hunches about what students struggle with, but they don't typically help us understand why students struggle.

Dr. Adam Gazzaley, professor of neurology, physiology, and psychiatry at the University of California, San Francisco, helped audience members understand the mechanics of this reality in his keynote address at the Learning and the Brain: Merging Minds and Technology Conference held in Boston, Massachusetts, in November 2017. Dr. Gazzaley compared the problems we encounter in medical assessments to those we experience in educational assessments. He suggested that in both fields, our targeting is weak, and this requires us to provide increased intervention, which increases the potential for side effects. Our tests are typically non-personalized and unimodal. Dr. Gazzaley reminds us that complex problems aren't resolved with simple solutions. Also, many tests run on an open loop: They don't increase our health, our knowledge, or our skills.

Tests like these simply measure performance, and they don't do it very well.

We need personalized assessments that enable precision targeting inside of closed-loop systems. In other words, our assessments must be customized to fit the unique learners we serve, and they must reward and challenge these learners in just-right ways rather than merely measuring performance. In an ideal assessment setting, teachers position themselves beside their students, making a careful study of their own learning as well. While Dr. Gazzaley and his colleagues are working on large-scale assessments that meet these criteria, most teachers have begun recognizing these problems and questioning their assessment practices, too. Many have found answers inside of a powerful practice called pedagogical documentation, which gives children a voice.

THE HACK: UNCOVER AND SHARE LEARNING STORIES

Stories matter. More than a tool to engage and entertain listeners, stories are teachers. They help us learn how to live in this world. They help us learn how to teach in it, too, particularly when the stories are grounded in meaningful data.

I struggle when educators denigrate the use of the term "data" in our field. It may be popular to reduce data to numbers, but this has never been a best practice. When we suggest that data-driven schools do harm to children, or at the very least, lack vision, we fail to communicate accurate and far more meaningful definitions of the word. Data themselves do no harm. How people choose to define and use data is often problematic, though.

Data is information. Numbers are one kind of information, but they're not the only kind of data that teachers rely on. Pedagogical documentation is driven by qualitative data and grounded in stories. Data includes anecdotal records, photographs, video and audio recordings, and the observations we make (even the ones we don't make notes about). When we define our passions and pursue them in the classroom, we are using data. When we invite our students to chase after their own passions, we're teaching them to do the same.

If you use any or all of these kinds of information to theorize and evolve your practice, you might be disappointed to learn that you are indeed a data-driven teacher. And when you suggest that being data-driven is something less than necessary, professional, or human, you might want to consider the unintended consequences of your words. Data matters. It matters because it helps students and teachers tell honest and inspiring learning stories, and these stories help us get under the hood of the testing machine.

Stories help us understand why learning happens and why it

doesn't in ways that are far more personalized and far better targeted. They have the potential to close the loops in our learning systems, too. When we use data to draft our stories, the results serve learners well. When we don't, our biases have a greater influence on our narratives. Begin to gather the right data and flip the script inside of your own classroom or school, especially if your school equates assessment with testing and data with numbers.

WHAT YOU CAN DO TOMORROW

My favorite fiction writing teacher once told me that a novel is really a collection of smaller stories called scenes which unfold in one specific time and place for a very specific purpose. I've come to think of assessment in a similar way. The assessment that we make of our student at year's end is informed one small scene at a time, as the days unfold and our studies of their learning and work evolve. The suggestions below will help you assess inside of one single scene of learning. You can try this tomorrow.

JUST AS A NOVEL IS COLLECTION OF SCENES, SO IS YOUR CAREER AS A TEACHER OF WRITING.

- **REFINE YOUR SHARED LEARNING TARGETS.**
  Define your targets with learners, taking their interests and needs into account. Be as precise as possible. If you are eager to know more about how well learners use evidence to support a claim,

unpack that target further. Which additional targets are tucked away inside of it? For example: How might students define evidence? Which research skills are they using to find it? Which criteria inform their understanding of quality evidence? Which processes do they use to connect evidence to the claim? The tighter the target, the more effective your assessment of writers will be. They'll self-assess better as well.

And there's more: When we know what our targets are, we're more willing to experiment with medium and modality. Arguments take many forms on the web and inside of our communities. Invite your students to play with contemporary forms, to mix and remix mediums, and to design new approaches for communicating their messages—based on what they know about their audience's interests and needs. The learning targets remain the same, regardless of how writers choose to connect with their audiences. Quality arguments include compelling claims that are worth making, evidence that supports the claim, an awareness of potential counterclaims, and evidence that refutes them. This form may be brought to life through a public service announcement, an editorial, or any number of other vehicles. What matters is that the claim is worth making, that it is made in a worthy way, and that the creator uses the medium and modality that is most likely to engage the audience.

- **ALIGN TARGETS, LESSON, INVESTIGATION, DRAFTING, FEEDBACK, REVISION.** Once you've defined a tight target, ensure that it aligns to your mini-lesson and any investigative work that writers will engage in. For example, if you're studying how well writers use the criteria of high-quality evidence to evaluate their sources, ensure that your lesson supports this target, and that when writers sink into independent work time, they're making their learning visible. As they draft, they'll need to demonstrate how they're using quality sources, and your feedback and their iterations should attend to this target. It's this alignment between the learning target, the lesson, the investigation, drafting, feedback, and revision that moves writers and their writing forward along the path you've set for them.

  Detours are welcome, though. Remember that emergent curriculum design is clear about what must be done, to protect time for what might be done. The learning targets are your priorities. Determine what your students want to investigate, tinker with, and learn. Encourage their investigations. Notice their newfound expertise, and invite them to share it with others. If you're the teacher who fears technology because you'll never be a master of all the tools, this reminder is for you: Give your students the time they need to translate print into other mediums without the benefit of your direction. Let them communicate their messages using other modalities. It's not your job to teach them how. It's your job to make the space, provide access, and protect a bit of time for inquiry and innovation. Let them wrestle with the details. Let them fail. Your shared learning targets are your greatest priority. If you must control, focus your energies there. Let everything else be uncovered. Discovered. Messed with. This is how learning stories emerge.

- **ASSESS OVER THEIR SHOULDERS, AND LET THEM ASSESS YOU.** Rather than simply reacting to the writing dilemmas your students put in front of you, approach independent writing time by assessing each writer's progress toward your shared target in just one or two minutes.

  It looks something like this: Approach writers one at a time, peek over their shoulders and into their work with your identified target in mind, and assess their progress toward it. Offer one bit of criteria-specific feedback relevant to their strengths, and then, rather than directing improvement, pose a question that will help each writer improve. Share a strategy if you have a helpful one to offer. Then, track their progress toward the target by using a simple scale like the one I've shared in image 9.1.

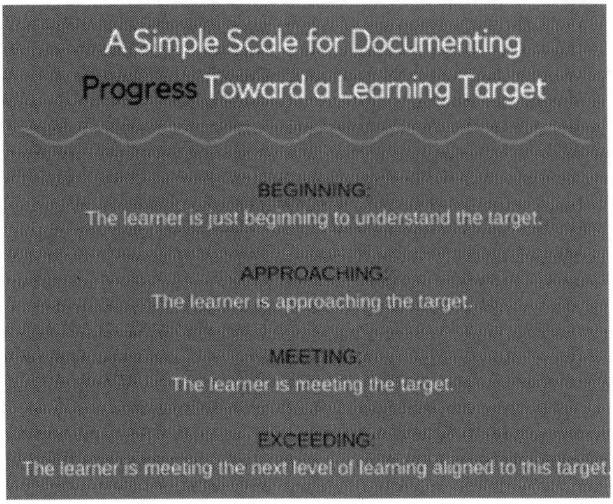

Image 9.1: A simple scale for documenting progress toward a target

As I mentioned in Hack I, it can be rewarding to invite your students to assess you as well. Remind them of your intentions as a teacher that day. Ask them to give you a criteria-specific feedback that feels warm, and then ask them what you can do better during the next session. Invite them to share their ideas and strategies. I typically use a ticket out the door to gather this information from writers. Anonymity and discretion helps writers feel more at ease with the work.

- **WORK WITH WRITERS TO DOCUMENT THEIR LEARNING, RELATIVE TO THE TARGET.** Invite them to share with you their learning and their growth toward the target. Encourage self-awareness, and coach them to document and study their progress. Photographs, audio recordings of interviews and conferences, and videos all work well here. Help your students understand what it looks like when a grade-level target is met, when they're approaching the target, and when they're just beginning to understand what the target means and how to achieve it. For those who are ready, introduce them to higher grade-level expectations, too.

- **MAKE TIME FOR REFLECTION.** Several years ago, I began leaving a minute or two open at the end of class for daily reflection. I shared prompts (see Image 9.2) with writers at the start of our year, explaining that each day they would choose one prompt to respond to in their writing notebooks after reviewing the evidence of learning they had documented throughout the day. Reflecting scene by scene inside of our workshop helped writers understand assessment as a verb rather than a noun, and stringing those reflections together ahead of our formal conferences empowered writers to show up motivated to lead and sustain powerful conversations about their learning and growth.

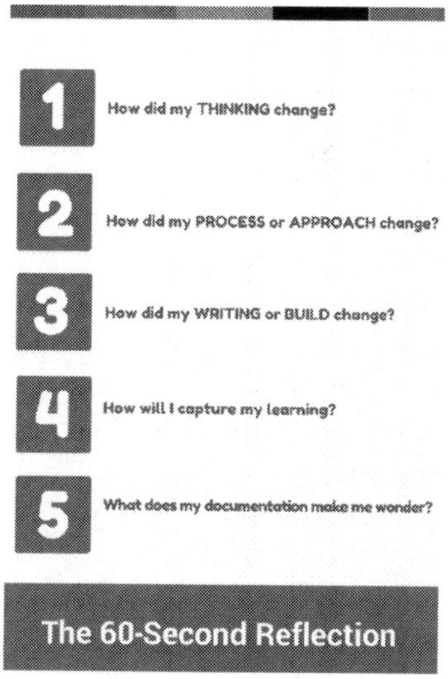

1 How did my THINKING change?

2 How did my PROCESS or APPROACH change?

3 How did my WRITING or BUILD change?

4 How will I capture my learning?

5 What does my documentation make me wonder?

The 60-Second Reflection

Image 9.2: Reflection is a powerful assessment tool.

A BLUEPRINT FOR FULL IMPLEMENTATION

Just as a novel is a collection of scenes, so is your career as a teacher of writing. Have you ever wondered what you could learn about your students and yourself by studying a collection of scenes captured from inside of your workshop? How might you use that data to craft a more significant story about the writers you serve and your own learning? What bonds each scene to the next? What holds them all together? What is most profound about your work? What matters most to your students? Which challenges remain timeless? What are you longing to improve about your practice? Here's how you might begin to find the answers to those questions:

Step 1: Define what you will study and how you will study it.

Explore what you are eager to learn about your students, yourself as a teacher of writing, your curriculum design, instruction, and assessment. Full implementation is a significant commitment. You need to love what you're studying. You need to be rewarded by the work, and so do your students. Find what matters most.

My first book, *Make Writing*, was a learning story that emerged from my foray into Grounded Theory research methodology. My approach was qualitative. I spent a long time documenting everything I could relevant to engagement in the writing workshops I led and in the classrooms where I taught beside other writing teachers. I didn't disrupt learning in order to test students, but instead I used my cell phone to capture photos, videos, audio recordings, and annotations. Scenes unfolded in primary, elementary, middle, and high school classrooms. I taught in rural and urban settings. I studied incredibly privileged kids, as well as those who lived in abject poverty.

I wasn't sure what I was looking for, and that was a good thing. I let the data that emerged from my work ground my theories. If you're eager to learn more about this methodology, drop into the supplemental resources folder for this Hack. You'll find a guidance document that will ease you into a simple start. You may choose to pursue a guiding question instead, or perhaps begin your study with an investigation of professional literature. There are advantages to each of these approaches, and only you can determine which approach feels right for you.

Once you've made this decision, define the moments that call for documentation. Choose your methods, then prepare your tools. You'll want them at the ready. Use the planning chart in Image 9.3.

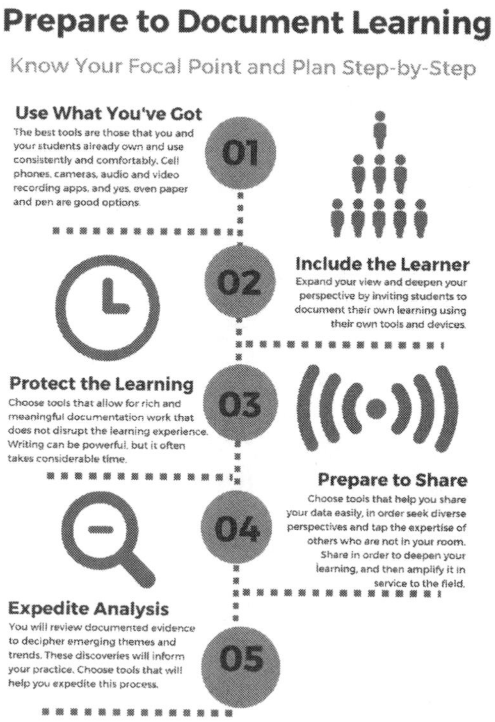

Prepare to Document Learning
Know Your Focal Point and Plan Step-by-Step

Use What You've Got
The best tools are those that you and your students already own and use consistently and comfortably. Cell phones, cameras, audio and video recording apps, and yes, even paper and pen are good options.

01

Include the Learner
Expand your view and deepen your perspective by inviting students to document their own learning using their own tools and devices.

02

Protect the Learning
Choose tools that allow for rich and meaningful documentation work that does not disrupt the learning experience. Writing can be powerful, but it often takes considerable time.

03

Prepare to Share
Choose tools that help you share your data easily, in order seek diverse perspectives and tap the expertise of others who are not in your room. Share in order to deepen your learning, and then amplify it in service to the field.

04

Expedite Analysis
You will review documented evidence to decipher emerging themes and trends. These discoveries will inform your practice. Choose tools that will help you expedite this process.

05

Image 9.3

Step 2: Document your learning.

Acting as a learner, documentarian, and participant in the assessment process can be overwhelming. At times, it's hard to know if evidence will be valuable in a moment. Know your purpose, gather what seems relevant, and know that you can grab more data later if necessary. Keep your evidence in an easily accessible place.

Step 3: Discover the stories within your findings.

Once you've gathered abundant data from the diverse scenes that will comprise the whole of your story, begin coding it. Review your evidence, keeping an open mind about what you notice. Often, the discoveries will be unexpected—embrace this. Assign simple codes in the form of letters, words, or numbers to specific trends and themes that you see emerging, and apply them consistently. You'll find tools and examples of my own work in the supplemental resources folder for this Hack.

Step 4: Theorize, based on evidence.

As you notice recurring patterns across multiple data points, cluster these findings and create a category for them. Consider how your categories and the data that live inside of them might inform your thinking, learning, and work. Find the emerging theories.

Step 5: Test your theories, and learn more.

Share what you're learning with others—including your students. Test your theories, gather more data, and refine your thinking as you go. This is how we remain lifelong learners inside of the field of education. This is how we come to know and do better.

OVERCOMING PUSHBACK

This is going to take too much time. That was my greatest worry when I began. I wanted to learn more about engagement in writing workshops, so I began by documenting everything, using efficient methods and tools that didn't disrupt teaching or learning. I started small, chose a meaningful topic, and kept my phone fully charged and in my pocket. It became my best documentation friend. I also accepted the fact that my work would unfold in fits and starts, over the course of an entire year. I knew that there would be peaks and valleys in my process, and sometimes, they were influenced by the amount of time I had available for the work. My students' immediate needs always came first.

Numbers matter most to my administrators, and some parents and students prefer them, too. This is understandable. I'm hoping that improving teaching and learning matters to these stakeholders as well, especially since this is the only way to improve those numbers, right? Test results can't tell us much about why learners perform the way that they do or how to help them make strides. Assessing on our feet, and documenting and studying learning, both provide powerful perspectives. Show the naysayers the value of your data and evidence of improved learning—both with and without numbers.

How do I report progress to parents? Rely on mode, rather than averaging grades. When we know our standards and our refined targets, it becomes easier to understand how learners are performing and why they are performing as they are. Targets help writing teachers become far more diagnostic. They give us sharper eyes and a keener intuition. They also help us report progress honestly and with greater specificity.

This was the case when I attended my first parent-teacher conference in my daughter's school on the heels of their shift to standards-based grading. Rather than receiving some general words of praise or shallow perspectives about the improvements she could make, I sat across the table from Nina, my daughter, and she shared her learning story with me. She pointed to work samples, reflected on her learning, and spoke to the charts on the walls of the classroom.

Rather than receiving an average, her teacher spoke with me about her progress toward their shared learning targets. She showed me a series of assessments that were captured during instruction. Nina's learning was never disrupted to capture these data. Her teacher scooped them from the experience itself, and what she gathered was revealing.

I left that conference with a clearer understanding of my daughter's writing habits, the specific knowledge she gained that year, and the skills she was perfecting. Her report card demonstrated how close she was to meeting prioritized standards. It was based on how often she achieved certain levels of proficiency relative to that target over time. The report card was standards-based, but it's possible to use these same approaches even if you're required to use traditional reporting methods.

To learn more about this approach or explore materials that can help you get started, visit the supplemental resources folder for this Hack.

I want someone to hand me a program and tell me what to do. That's easy enough, and believe me, I can empathize. Teaching writing is tough, scary, and exhausting stuff, but here's the reality: Once you have that program and others tell you what to do, you'll still need to assess, gather data, analyze your findings, and embrace all the uncertainty that helps you know better if you're ever going to do better. Great writing teachers are made over the course of an entire career, not inside a single scene or even a hundred scenes that unfold over an entire year. So, adopt a program if you'd like, or adapt someone else's plan, but let your assessment findings light your pathway. It's the only way to ensure that the program you've chosen is meeting the needs of the children you serve.

THE HACK IN ACTION

I've loved showcasing other teachers and the writers they support. Whenever I do this, they make connections. Teachers who did not know one another recognize the kindred spirits that appear across these pages, and friendships are fostered online and on the ground. This is why I decided to keep many of my own stories off the page as I drafted this second *Hack Learning* book. As you've seen, there were a few that I needed to tell, though, and this is another one of them.

I often think about my former students—the ones I taught long before I learned to be a learner. I've now spent over a decade teaching beside teachers and blogging about my practice. I present at conferences and write books about my learning. I'm connected to inspiring educators on Facebook and Twitter and LinkedIn. I love my work, and while I may not be confident in my ability to always do what's best, I'm confident in my commitment to figuring it all out.

This makes me a different person than I was way back when my students filed into their seats, flipped open their notebooks, and awaited my performance at the front of the room. I daresay they wouldn't recognize me now, and I know that I owe all of them an apology.

The fact is that when I was in the classroom, I didn't know the importance of assessment and feedback. I didn't know how to look deeply into student work, offer good feedback, or intervene. I was too busy teaching curriculum to teach kids: getting stuff done, assigning things, grading them, making assumptions.

What a disaster.

For instance, back then it wasn't uncommon for me to teach a mini-lesson about constructing a claim and then peek over my students' shoulders just long enough to get annoyed by their lack of paragraphing. Rather than aligning my feedback to the target, which was also the center of my mini-lesson, I corrected their paragraphing instead. They revised in response to that feedback, and then I would wonder why their claims were so weak. Hadn't I taught an entire lesson to support that target? Didn't I spend several days talking at them about this? What was the matter with them anyway?

Too many years would pass before I began aligning my learning target with my mini-lesson teaching point, the feedback I provided, and the revision focal points that writers established. When I did, everything changed for the better.

Here's my point: Assessment isn't merely a tool that allows us to study a writer's progress. Assessments make us better teachers. They help us grow, too.

This was the case in Buffalo, New York, where elementary teachers began studying how their shifting instructional practices were influencing student writing performance at the start of a new school year. Journey mapping positioned them as learners from the outset, helping them capture stories from the first point of contact through the entire writing process. Journey maps often take the form of infographics, and may use items such as long strips of chart paper, markers, and sticky notes. They make for dynamic work. To see examples of journey maps and learn how to use them, visit the supplemental resources folder for this Hack. You'll find a bunch of them plus a few protocols waiting for you.

Teachers began by sharing what they wished to achieve and what their greater intentions were (if known) for their first writing units. Thinking about how writers move through the process helped them identify opportunities to enrich the experience. It also helped them anticipate stretches of rough road, including gaps in necessary knowledge and skills, as well as moments within the process where they predicted that writers might experience overwhelm, frustration, and even breakdown.

When teachers mapped the emotional journey that they predicted their students would take, they gained important insight. Each identified one potential student struggle that they wished to crack open, explore, and remedy. They determined how they would document learning during this phase with their students, and agreed to bring these data and the greater stories that would surround them back to the table the next time they met, in order to analyze their findings and refine their hunches about students' needs. Their work began uncertainly and with many false starts. But these teachers remained committed to forward movement, and even the most overwhelmed among them made strides with assessment and documentation. They even added a pre- and post-assessment process to their unit plans, so they could gather better information about how their instruction affected growth.

Now, when teachers need to make balanced and informed decisions about the writers they support, they're better able to triangulate their data. Rather than relying on standardized test scores alone, they refer to the qualitative data captured throughout the process, as well as baseline and post-assessment writing samples, authentic writing completed throughout the process, and evidence gathered from their exchanges on the ground with writers.

When we uncover and share learning stories, everyone inside of our workshop thrives. This is a practice that can and should replace testing and evaluation inside of every writing classroom. It should also replace those professional learning approaches that fail to move writers and teachers forward. The materials in the supplemental resources folder for this Hack will help you begin this work. There, you will find:

- Guidance for using Grounded Theory as a beginner

- Protocols for coding qualitative data well

- Approaches for making learning visible

Image 9.4: Scan the code to find supplemental resources for supporting Hack 9.

HACK 10

FRAME BETTER FEEDBACK

Cultivating confidence and capacity

Alas, too few people understand what feedback is and isn't.
— GRANT WIGGINS, EDUCATOR, AUTHOR, VISIONARY

THE PROBLEM: CONFUSING FEEDBACK
WITH COMPLIMENTS AND CRITICISM

D O YOU REMEMBER the first time anyone sat and spoke with you seriously about your writing? I do. I don't remember what the work was, and I don't remember what was said. I remember how my teacher's thoughtful attention made me feel, though. He helped me feel competent. He also helped me realize that my work, while imperfect, mattered. This made me want to improve it.

Most important, my teacher didn't tell me how to make my work better. Instead, he helped me identify very clear purposes for my work, and he shared with me a variety of ideas and possibilities relevant to those targets. He didn't position himself as an expert that I needed to obey. Rather, he was my collaborator. He trusted my capabilities and respected my expertise. He knew I'd figure it out.

This approach made me a writer, and it's made me a teacher, too.

Feedback is useful to learners when their purposes are clear, the timing is right, and the information shared is criteria-specific and empowers growth. Compliments and criticism may be offered in a timely manner, but they aren't always aligned to the writer's purposes, they often lack specificity, and both typically fail to empower growth. Compliments merely validate what writers have already done, while criticism, even when it is criteria-specific, tends to shame them.

Compliments and criticism undermine the kind of trust that we work so hard to cultivate inside of our workshops. When our work is greeted with enthusiastic affirmations, we can't help but wonder if the speaker is merely being kind, while criticism is often felt as an assault on our person, whether or not this was anyone's intention. Both make it difficult to know for certain if our work is truly valued. Or, for that matter, if we are. Here's what's worse: When people are groomed to provide compliments, feedback often starts to feel like criticism as well. When this happens, no one benefits.

Future-ready writing workshops are facilitated by those who know how to help writers set and maintain high expectations for themselves and others while remaining sensitive to their complex social and emotional needs. Compassion is currency inside of these spaces, and it's rooted in the way that people speak to one another. While compliments and criticism do little to enhance workshop culture or the work that writers produce, certain feedback protocols, such as peer review, show great promise.

THE HACK: FRAME BETTER FEEDBACK

Peer review is one of my favorite because it coaches the development of warm and cool feedback.

Warm feedback isn't a compliment: It's an opportunity for writers to learn where they've begun to meet a learning target that matters to them, or where they are about to meet a target. Cool feedback isn't criticism: It's a prompt that helps writers think differently or deeper about their priori- tized learning targets, what they've already written, and what they could do next, to achieve their visions.

WRITERS NEED TO RECEIVE FEEDBACK IN THE MOMENT THAT IS MOST USEFUL TO THEM.

When we use warm and cool frames to provide feedback, writers retain ownership of their work and emerge from the trans- action with new perspectives and ideas that will help them improve. Those ideas are typically self- generated, too. Reviewers are coached to offer questions rather than offering directives or advice, and they do so within a care- fully protocoled experience that leaves everyone feeling heard and supported.

Teachers can learn much about supporting writers well by par- ticipating in quality peer review themselves, and committing to the use of warm and cool feedback rather than compliments or criticism in diverse contexts. I became acquainted with the peer review process, captured in image 10.1, as a fellow of Communities for Learning: Leading Lasting Change®.

Peer Review

The Protocol	Considerations
Before you begin, divide the total amount of time available for review by the number of writers in the group. This will ensure equal time for all.	Warm feedback is not a compliment. Consider the type of feedback requested and use evidence from the work to suggest where the writer is meeting goals or demonstrating a readiness to.
1. The writer under review shares a selected piece of writing or a dilemma.	
2. The writer asks for a specific kind of feedback or support.	Cool feedback is not criticism. Pose targeted questions that provoke deeper or different thinking about the work.
3. Reviewers read the work or listen to it as it is read aloud.	
4. Reviewers take up to five minutes to plan warm and cool feedback.	
5. Reviewers share warm feedback first, taking care to share just one thought at a time, in rounds, ensuring that all reviewers have an opportunity to contribute. Once an individual's feedback is exhausted, he or she may pass a turn. Once warm feedback rounds are complete, reviewers may repeat the process, providing cool.	Sometimes, reviewers struggle to find just-right words. Consider using high quality rubrics and sentence frames to guide your review.
	Remember, feedback is a service writers provide to one another, not a set of expectations that must be met. No need to explain, justify or defend the work.
6. When peer review is complete, all copies are returned to the writer.	

Image 10.1

Founded and facilitated by Dr. Giselle O. Martin-Kniep, Joanne Picone-Zocchia, and Dr. Diane Cunningham, this professional learning community recognizes the importance of quality feedback and coaches it with great intention. This is where I learned that being a great educator calls us to pursue far more than the development of our own expertise. Being a great educator calls us to help others uncover and nurture their own expertise.

Protocols enable this by ensuring inclusivity and equity for all participants. They provide clear constraints, including specific time limits, expectations for speakers and listeners, group sizes, prompts, materials, and steps to be followed. Using them well requires practice, self-assessment, and a good deal of reflection. It's been my experience that teachers who use protocols for their own professional or personal learning purposes gain experience that also serves their students well. It's difficult to appreciate the power of any protocol until you've used it yourself. This is especially true of feedback protocols. You'll find examples of my favorites for writers of all ages and experience levels in the supplemental resources folder for this Hack.

WHAT YOU CAN DO TOMORROW

Feedback is an area where you can start making improvements right away, without too much time or effort. Below are my ideas to get you started tomorrow.

- **MAKE IT TIMELY.** Writers need to receive feedback in the moment that is most useful to them. Adding feedback to final drafts? Not very useful. In fact, by the time a first draft is complete, writers have already worked through dozens of micro-revisions and more substantive ones as well. This is why I advocate for blocking forms and writing bit by bit—toward specific targets. This approach enables teachers to peek over shoulders and provide manageable morsels of relevant feedback every day as writers work independently.

- **DISTINGUISH FEEDBACK FROM COMPLIMENTS AND CRITICISM.** Talk openly with writers about the unintended consequences of compliments and criticism, and distinguish both from feedback. Capture the differences on anchor charts, hang them on the wall in your classroom, and invite writers to reflect before they offer feedback to their peers.

- **USE SPECIFIC CRITERIA ALIGNED TO A CLEAR TARGET.** If everyone knows what the day's learning targets are, it will be easier to think clearly about degrees of proficiency, evidence of success, and common challenges that writers might face as they work their way toward the targets. This allows you to anticipate which feedback might be most helpful and offer it in just-right ways at just-right moments. There is nothing more challenging than looking into a piece of student work, noticing a thousand entry points for improvement, and having no idea how to help them begin. Targets help us prioritize and plan our approach. This elevates the quality of our talks with writers.

  Once your targets are clarified, you may still struggle to find just the right words when speaking to students about their work. You'll find targeted feedback frames in the supplemental resources folder for this Hack. Use them and share them with your students. They'll appreciate the guidance, too.

- **ANCHOR YOUR FEEDBACK TO EXAMPLES.** It's not enough to help writers recognize their strengths and needs. Most need feedback to be anchored to clear models that they can replicate. I'll be honest, though: I prefer it when teachers use their own writing to illustrate craft and process moves. It's much easier to produce a writing sample that is closely aligned to your needs, and when you write beside your students, they lean in and listen hard. Writing is risky stuff. The braver you are, the more they'll pay attention, and the more you'll learn about teaching writing well.

- **COACH STUDENTS TO ASK FOR AND PROVIDE HIGH-QUALITY FEEDBACK.** Define warm and cool feedback explicitly, and use a protocol that is considerate of your writers' experience and age levels. The protocol in image 10.1 is useful with high school writers, but you'll find adaptations for primary, intermediate, and middle school writers in the supplemental resources folder for this Hack. Anticipate false starts and less than ideal applications at first. As writers engage in peer review, position yourself as a learner, and document what you notice. Pay attention to how writers ask for feedback, how reviewers plan what they will say, and how carefully teams honor the protocol. How might you help them become better feedback providers? What will your next lesson attend to?

A BLUEPRINT FOR FULL IMPLEMENTATION

Becoming a great provider of feedback is an art, and it takes dedicated practice to improve. Invite students to provide feedback to one another daily, even if it's just a quick bit of warm reflection. Don't throw the entire protocol at them all at once, either. Teach it bit by bit, and adjust your instruction as their needs and interests emerge. The following steps will help you scaffold writers toward success. It won't come easily, but if you're mindful and intentional in your practice, you will sustain the gains.

Step 1: Start small.

First, begin with a brief mini-lesson on warm feedback. Tell a story about your own experiences with it, define it, and help your students understand what warm feedback looks like and sounds like as well as how people typically feel when they're receiving it. Add these criteria to an anchor chart that writers can return to. You'll find my own as well as other peeks into my peer review groups inside of the supplemental resources folder for this Hack. Once you're confident that students have mastered warm feedback that is specific to a target, repeat the process to introduce cool feedback in the same way.

Step 2: Assess progress.

I often ask writers to plan the feedback they intend to provide on a note catcher like the one you see in image 10.2.

Figure 10.2: Planning, sharing, and reflecting
on the quality of our feedback

This enables writers to pause and thoughtfully craft what they intend to say while also making their thinking visible. I appreciate seeing how my students assess their peers' work and more important, how they frame their assessment in a way that is kind, criteria-specific, and motivating. What I discover from these assessments guides the mini-lessons that immediately follow. This raises another important point: Inviting your students to assess the quality of their peer review is powerful stuff, too. Ask them:

How did peer review go today? How might we make it better next time? I often collect responses as a ticket out the door, and I'm always glad when I do. Kids are honest, and when they're asked, they provide their teachers powerful feedback.

Step 3: Intervene.

As writers review one another's work, listen in on their exchanges. When necessary, push pause on any group's peer review, and invite them to listen as you reframe a compliment or a bit of criticism. This is how they will learn to do the same.

If writers aren't honoring the protocol, such as if the writers whose work is under review disrupt the exchange by qualifying the decisions that he or she made or by adding a ton of unnecessary context, remind them that peer review is a silent protocol: The person whose work is under review must remain silent throughout. This is critical, as it promotes actively listening, protects what limited time is available for all to receive a review, and reinforces the fact that peer review is a gift. It's a service that reviewers provide to writers, and there is no expectation that writers will act on the feedback. Since this is the case, there is no need to explain, justify, or defend the work. It's enough to simply listen and then decide what we will do with the feedback provided to us.

Step 4: Diversify your tools.

Consider moving peer review into digital spaces. I've experimented with this quite a bit and studied the effect. Writers who are reluctant to share face to face are often very willing to share online, and those who struggle to plan and provide great feedback on their feet often tell me that they prefer having more time and the ability to rethink and revise their statements. Digital tools enable this. Finally, when we share our feedback online, writers are better able to return to it, and so are you. You'll find examples of different kinds of exchanges in different digital spaces in the supplemental resources folder for this hack.

Step 5: Grow your sphere of influence.

It's hard to create compassionate workshop cultures inside of systems that unintentionally undermine our efforts. Start courageous conversations with your colleagues and leaders about the influence of feedback on learning and performance. Share the protocols you value, and invite them to join you in your commitment to providing warm and cool feedback rather than compliments or criticism. Perhaps you'll find, like many teachers that I support, that this single shift in how people speak to one another has a profound effect on motivation, morale, and culture.

OVERCOMING PUSHBACK

Cool feedback is kind, but kids need to learn how to deal with criticism. I agree: Kids do need to learn how to deal with criticism, because not everyone is privy to the power of feedback protocols, and even those who are will slip into a critical stance from time to time. I find that knowledge is one of the best antidotes for criticism, and writers gain much of it when they begin to internalize the criteria that define the craft and process of writing. Peer review doesn't make writers soft. It makes them sharp—sharp enough to know when criticism is coming from an informed perspective and when it isn't. Something else: Cool feedback, by its very nature, inspires us to get informed. When we're required to review someone's work closely enough to frame questions about it, we learn a great deal. Criticism is often reactive and driven by bias. Cool feedback is informed, and it's anchored to a shared learning target.

My students don't respond to the feedback that I offer, so I'm not going to waste my time providing it. Before you give up, think about changing your timing and/or your modality. There is nothing more frustrating than spending hours of your free time writing carefully constructed feedback on student work, only to have them toss it in the garbage can. I empathize completely. What if you started talking with kids informally about their work as it's in process? What if you put your written feedback on the first draft rather than the last? What if you dropped your feedback into Google Docs or created peer review groups in Voxer or Flipgrid? What if you added your voice to the group? What if feedback felt more like a helpful conversation rather than an evaluation?

I teach at the secondary level and my class sizes are huge, which makes providing high-quality feedback almost impossible. This is something I have struggled with. There were two approaches that made things more manageable for me, in addition to blocking forms and writing and reviewing bit by bit. The first involved creating staggered assessment cycles, and the second involved affinity mapping student drafts.

Staggered assessment cycles typically function like this: Assign a different draft collection day for each section that you teach. This way, you will only need to provide feedback on the work of one section at a time, and no one will be waiting too long to hear back from you. Also, if you've been providing feedback bit by bit throughout the process, writers will be submitting significantly improved drafts that you're already familiar with. This eases the process.

When we affinity map with student drafts, we use the following scale to quickly skim and then cluster their drafts:

- Work that is exceeding the expectations of your shared learning targets

- Work that is meeting the expectations of your shared learning targets

- Work that is approaching the expectations of your shared learning targets

- Work that is significantly below the expectations of your shared learning targets

It's important that you eyeball the work quickly and then place it in a cluster rather than reviewing each paper carefully to craft precise feedback. Do not grade the work, and do not rely on your rubric just yet. Simply cluster the drafts you've collected.

Once you've created collections of work that share certain affinities, look into each collection, and define what is present in each cluster. What do you see in the work of the students who are exceeding expectations? What is present in work that meets expectations? How might you characterize the work of writers who are approaching the standards? What do you notice about the work that is significantly below your shared expectations? Focus on what is present, not what is missing. Create a criteria-specific profile for each cluster. Then ask yourself:

- Based on this evidence, how have these writers grown?

- Which elements of craft or phases of the process do I need to coach a bit better?

- Are there skills or bits of knowledge that every group could benefit from learning or revisiting? If so, how might I design a whole group mini-lesson?

- Which groups might benefit from a small guided writing lesson? How might I free up time to work with them?

Some of the teachers that I support in schools use a combination of teaching and writing bit by bit, over the shoulder feedback, staggered learning cycles, and affinity mapping to create a series of highly effective and tightly connected feedback loops. This enables them to review work far more often and much more efficiently. It also allows them to feed writers forward in ways that ensure the next review will require even less heavy lifting.

THE HACK IN ACTION

I founded the WNY Young Writers' Studio—Studio for short—in 1998. It's a makerspace for K-12 writers and teachers of writing, and anyone who has spent time there will tell you that peer review is the octane that fuels us. When I first introduced the protocol, I did so at the secondary level. We began by exploring warm feedback. I shared my own experiences, including the memory that framed the first paragraphs of this hack, and then I defined warm feedback. Explicitly. I used an anchor chart to distinguish warm feedback from compliments, criticism, and even cool feedback. I provided students sentence frames and planning tools. I scaffolded the work carefully, friends. I did.

And what happened?

Well, despite my careful planning and thoughtful reminders to provide warm feedback only, my students dove right in and started criticizing one another. Pointing out flaws. Directing revision. Breaking my heart.

Incidentally, this has happened nearly every time since then when I've introduced a new group to peer review. I've come to expect it now. And I'm also prepared. Now, as writers engage in peer review, I walk the room and listen. When it's clear that a group needs help, I push pause on their conversation and provide feedback on their feedback. Sometimes, I need to turn them toward the protocol because they aren't following it. At other times, I need to acknowledge their commendable intentions to provide quality warm feedback just before I reframe it in a way that meets our standards. Regardless of the reason, I find these exchanges productive. Writers tell me that they do, too.

Here's something else: Once I've identified strong feedback providers and peer review practitioners, I put them in positions of leadership. They're given the power to push pause in their own groups, and they're also invited to drop into elementary sessions to do the same. This is how we build capacity with compassion across our entire community.

Lake Shore High School English teachers are refining their feedback practices as well. As their students complete assessment drafts, we've begun meeting to collaboratively review them. They begin by affinity mapping—clustering the work samples according to their common levels of development—and then, defining what is present in each distinct cluster.

The last time we met to review the findings, I was impressed by their final reflections and especially, their action plans. Rather than simply marching through their curriculum, these teachers intended to respond to the evidence gleaned from the affinity mapping process. They identified issues that were plaguing writers across all levels of proficiency, issues that were specific to single clusters, and issues that only related to a handful of outliers, or perhaps just one single student. They adjusted their instructional plans accordingly.

All were willing to work with writers in small, guided, invitational groups. And all were eager to document the learning that unfolded inside of these groups. Most important, this department chose to step away from grading and evaluation long enough to embrace assessment, plan better feedback, and design uncommon intervention approaches, including writing and assessing bit by bit.

Imagine the difference these small shifts could make, if all high school teachers were as willing to embrace them.

When writers struggle, we want to know why, and we want to help them get better. Despite evidence to the contrary, too many of us still believe that grades provide insight and that standardized test scores suggest solutions.

This is understandable. Numbers provide a kind of quick certainty when we're feeling overwhelmed or frustrated. They seem more efficient to work with, too. Numbers disregard messy complexities. They're absolutes, and absolutes feel good. Whether we like what they suggest or not, numbers are definitive—providing answers that allow us to move beyond the discomfort of our uncertainty. Rather than dancing with the details, we can draw quick conclusions. This is simple. Easy. Painless.

The problem is that numbers fail to provide a pathway forward for writers, and the conclusions we draw from poorly targeted tests often do more harm than good.

Helping writers in honest and healthy ways is difficult work that opens everyone up to vulnerability. The fact is that if we're going to get real about gathering the data that matter and providing high-quality feedback to writers, our discomfort may have no end. At times, it may even deepen and intensify. We might make mistakes, and we won't have much to hide behind. Numbers are a screen. I'm grateful for the courageous teachers who are willing to cast it off. They set an important example. I wish I'd been as brave when I was still in the classroom.

I'm grateful to witness it on the daily now, though. Each day, I meet with teachers who are learning to talk with their students as a means of assessment. They're helping them talk with each other better, too. And everyone is starting to listen. This is how writers thrive. It's how humans thrive, too.

Visit the supplemental resources folder to begin this work yourself. Here's just a bit of what you'll find there:

- K-16 peer review protocols

- Charts to support the peer review process

- Targeted feedback frames

Image 10.3: Scan the code to find supplemental resources for supporting Hack 10.

CONCLUSION
Writers and teachers in the making

"**W**HAT ARE YOU making?" I asked Ava as I wound my way around the classroom peering over shoulders, examining drafts, and peeking at what makers were building. Our writing workshop session was drawing to a quick close, and it was clear that she'd made some impressive progress.

"I'm making a boat," she said. "The main character in my story is an amazing piano player, and she has to perform in a concert far away," she explained. "Only when she gets on the boat, she finds out that it isn't just any old boat. It's a special boat, driven by elves who are about to begin a quest."

Ava spoke quickly, her words rising like steam above a high

boil of ideas. I wondered how many of them came to her while building and which ones would find their way into her draft.

"So, how does making the boat help you as a writer?" I asked her, as I had asked several hundred other writers before her. This is what I want to know. It's what I have to learn.

"Well, I had to think hard about the way I was building it, because I wanted it to look like the one I was imagining," she began. "So, I tried to use the Lego pieces that would help me do that at first. But, my kit was full of lots of different kinds of pieces that didn't really connect with what I was imagining. I really wanted to use them, though. Playing around with them changed my first ideas about what the boat looked like."

"So the boat you made wasn't the boat you thought you would make," I wondered aloud. "Were you unhappy with your changes?"

"No," she shook her head vehemently. "Using the pieces that I had helped me create different details, and I like them even more. Do you remember how you taught us to list our ideas when we were brainstorming?"

"Of course I do," I said, recalling the teaching point of our last mini-lesson.

"Well, I'm adding what I notice about my boat to this list," she said, directing me to a page in the ideas section of her writer's notebook. "These details will help me make my writing better."

Several months later, as Ava was working on an entirely new writing project, I found her building something using scraps of cardboard from our recycling bin. I knew that she was deep into the drafting phase at this point in her process. I also knew that she was feeling a bit stuck.

"That's why I'm making this," she explained. "I'm building what will happen next because I'm not sure how to write it."

"So, how does building help you figure out what to write?" I wondered aloud.

"I don't have to know *everything* about the next part to start building. I just have to build *something*. Then, once I start, I usually want to add more to it or make something new that connects with it," she told me.

"And that probably gives you new ideas to write about, too," I realized.

"Yes, it can," she said confidently, and I was validated by her authority.

I remember becoming a writer in the quiet of my bedroom, tucked under my bedsheets with a flashlight, pencil, and paper in hand. I wrote stories because I didn't have any left on my shelf to read. My mother took me to the library often, but I quickly tore through every title I borrowed, and without stories, my life was pretty lonely. So, when I ran out of books, I wrote my own.

How sad I was for the other children in our sleepy little town who didn't like to write but instead preferred building dollhouses with their fathers or pinning patterns to fabric before slicing it into parts that would eventually be sewn whole. Little did I know about making or design thinking, back then. Little did I know about what it meant to make a story instead of writing one.

I carried my ignorance into the classroom a decade later, where I coaxed angsty teenagers into the chairs and convinced them to begin putting print down on paper. The room was silent while I waited on drafts, and our conferences felt more like mandated check-ins than lingering conversations. I sensed that I was supposed to be certain, and that this mattered more than curiosity to most.

How strange it is to know less and wonder more, with each passing year.

Today, writers make and break and tinker and play inside of my workshops. I share what I can and own what I can't. I ask far too many questions, and take way too many pictures. Then, I spill the results across my kitchen table and look for the thread that ties each scene—each story—to the next.

I'm learning as I go, writing beside my students, and making new discoveries along the way. I've let go of the need to know and I've embraced the opportunity to discover. Most important, I'm helping other writing teachers do the same.

The world is such a different place than when I was young. It will be even less predictable next year. I don't know about you, but I'm realizing that if I'm to make any difference in this world, it won't be in the delivery of content, skills, or expectations, but instead in the example I set and pathways I illuminate for those who are counting on me to lead. What will matter is how I respond when they choose to move off course.

Future-ready writing workshops are built on frameworks that bend, so as not to break. They produce writers and teachers who do the same. So, I invite you to teach by design. Document your learning. Engage others in your story, and share your growing expertise. Embrace every opportunity to wonder with a purpose, and give the writers that you support the permission to do the same. Learn how to communicate without print, and let your students know this matters. Show them how this matters.

Some stories are too big for words, so invite your students to make them, instead. Watch them as they work. Ask them every question that you might need them to answer. And then, lean in and listen hard. This is how they'll make you a teacher.

If the ideas I've shared compel or confound you, I hope you'll find me on Twitter @AngelaStockman. You'll find me in the #makewriting stream. I'd love to hear your story. I'd love to be a part of it going forward, too.

PREVIEW ANGELA STOCKMAN'S
MAKE WRITING

HACK 3

TEACH THEM TO TINKER

Play Through the Process

It is a happy talent, to know how to play.
—Ralph Waldo Emerson, Poet/Lecturer

THE PROBLEM: WRITERS STRUGGLE TO
GENERATE AND DEVELOP CREATIVE IDEAS

As a young teacher, I was perpetually hunting for perfect writing prompts, strategies, and tools, certain that if I asked the ideal question, provided the right graphic organizer, orchestrated the best set of strategies, I'd help my students generate and execute enticing ideas.

These efforts brought me some small measure of success. I could often get my kids writing, and when they followed my lead what emerged was often accurate, if uninspired. Getting them to persevere through the process was far more challenging than I ever imagined, though.

Eager to unlock the secret to sustaining their momentum, I began studying the writers who not only invested themselves from the start, but who maintained their stamina throughout the process. I noticed that these writers invested significantly more time in idea generation, and they often employed strategies that were different from those I taught them. It was clear that those who planned their writing struggled less; however, these same writers told me that the graphic organizers I required were confining.

My most invested writers were quietly but fiercely independent. They generated their own processes for accomplishing things, and they often kept this hidden from me. They were eager to please, but self-aware enough to know that pleasing me had little to do with their growth.

These writers often augmented the strategies that I provided or avoided using them altogether unless they were required to do so. They also made creative use of the resources at their disposal and sought out others on their own.

THE HACK: TEACH THEM TO TINKER

When we make writing, we tear things down, break them apart, build, test, and reconstruct as we go. Like makers, writers work with many moving, interdependent parts, and while our spaces are filled with containers that hold supplies, the containers we depend on most are those that house our ideas. These are the same containers that make our thinking and our knowledge visible. Tangible. Mobile.

More than any prompt, organizer, or strategy that I assign, the spaces, supplies, and tools I provide serve as catalysts for new ideas and remedies for the dilemmas that writers face. When I was a new teacher, my lessons helped students write efficiently and proficiently. My goals are very different now. Experience has taught me that talented writers are far more than efficient or proficient. They're adept.

CHARACTERIZING THE ADEPT WRITER

While many writers begin the process by sketching outlines and filling out graphic organizers, adept writers often begin by tearing other texts apart. They break down the work that inspires them, studying how it works so they can mimic an expert's approach. While these initial efforts might feel unsatisfyingly derivative, modifying existing frameworks typically inspires the development of texts that are legitimately original.

Writers who become adept are distinct in another way: Rather than approaching the process as a routine or a set of defined steps, they move through it in a recursive fashion. Most notably, they *tinker* during each phase of the writing. When writers tinker, they often make their writing moveable, crafting it on index cards or sticky notes, slicing their drafts into pieces, and isolating portions of their work from the whole in order to study and play with them.

> Approaching writing as a continuous process forwarded by efficient movement from one step to the next often fails to help writers discover anything new about themselves or their work. If they are to remain invested, novice writers need to reap far greater rewards. Deep processing satiates, and tinkering is what enables it.

Adept writers are not satisfied by plans that result in the tidy production of drafts. They strive to surface the unexpected, and they generate multiple ideas and options before selecting the best path. They aim for complexity, playing with the possibilities that emerge from the process, often shaping and reshaping their vision as they draft deeper into their work. These writers go well beyond merely getting the job done.

This is how magic happens, and magic is what writers are after. They get it. Writing isn't merely a means to an end such as publication. Writing is a richly rewarding end in itself. Tinkering empowers writers to elevate the quality of their writing as they go. This is how they become expert craftsmen.

Revisiting the Writing Process

A writer's recognition of alternative approaches and eagerness to test and learn from them may account for some distinction between adept and less dexterous writers. To foster this understanding, we can begin simply by questioning the most popular models of the writing process and casting a critical eye over what these models make visible versus what remains concealed.

In its traditional form, the writing process appears to be linear: prewriting, drafting, revising, editing, and publishing. While such a model conceptualizes writing simply and clearly, it is decidedly misleading and has provoked serious misinterpretation. The process is not sequential, nor is it tidy, and when writers are initiated into their work in this way, the expertise they gain is likely superficial at best.

Other renditions of the process liken it to a synergistic web rather than a series of steps. While these models promote a more accurate representation of the process, they fall short in another significant way: They only lay the surface of it bare. The magic of the process remains concealed.

Familiarity with writers and writing has taught me that there is no one way to experience the writing process. It is a multifarious and ever-shifting enterprise. While models can help us develop a sense of what happens for most writers, they cannot represent the various ways individual writers move into and out of phases, nor do they establish set patterns for the actions and types of thinking writers do during the process.

I've learned that much can be gained from asking writers to define and sketch their own models rather than imposing one on them. Consider your own process: What does it typically look like? Do you always begin by brainstorming ideas, or do you prefer to leap right into drafting? Are you a planner, or do you prefer to let your stories surprise you? I share my own process before I ask such questions, in order to distinguish doodling and sketching from pursuing high art. Since my intention is to support rather than direct writers, asking them to make their processes transparent is a powerful entry point into that work.

This approach helped me discover something important: It's interesting to compare how writers move from one state in their processes to the next, but what happens at the intersection of states is incredibly compelling, and so is the transformation in thinking that I witness when writers strive to make what happens there apparent.

Writing can sometimes seem like an ethereal endeavor, but self-awareness makes us masters of our own experiences. The most masterful and satisfied writers I know share one commonality: Regardless of how they approach the process, when they speak about what happens in the intersection of states, their descriptions are reminiscent of tinkering.

What's tinkering?

Tinkering with writing involves messing around with one small excerpt or one experience in the process, testing various strategies or approaches before committing to any one of them, and often experiencing happy surprises along the way.

When we tinker, we approach writing as an act of discovery. Our intent isn't to merely master craft, but to illuminate the process, to uncover our relationship with it, and notice how our productivity, our artistry, and even our abilities to persevere are affected.

New writers are often taught that revision takes place after drafting. Some distinguish it from editing, but many do not, and the resulting thinking and work are often less than gratifying. Approaching writing as a continuous process forwarded by efficient movement from one step to the next often fails to help writers discover anything new about themselves or their work. If they are to remain invested, novice writers need to reap far greater rewards. Deep processing satiates, and tinkering is what enables it.

Tinkering happens in each state of the writing process, regardless of how we move through it. The process can be recursive or even repetitive, depending on the level of satisfaction writers gain as they work it. Sometimes we need to revisit certain parts and work them differently to achieve the result we're hoping for. At other times, we need to cycle through most states multiple times. This requires patience on the part of the writer and restraint on the part of the teacher.

I've found it necessary to adjust my expectations, particularly concerning the production of original work, which requires scaffolding. In other words, the first time through a process, writers might rely heavily on the ideas and inspiration they gained from reading another writer's works. They practice creative theft, stealing with integrity, and modifying existing texts and frameworks to create their own. As writers gain experience and have the opportunity to tinker and test varied approaches, their ideas and the resulting text transform into authentic expertise.

A variety of tools enable this evolution, including index cards, sticky notes, notebooks, interactive charts, paper scrolls, foam boards, and grids. The purpose is to isolate ideas so we can move them around and situate them beside one another, creating new contexts and possibilities.

Notebooks, binders, and mind maps are important containers for independent writing efforts. Meaningful spaces, interactive displays, and anchor charts enable collaborative learning and play. Writers consistently participate in both kinds of experiences. Sticky notes and index cards enable transport, too: When writers record the thoughts, ideas, and bits of knowledge generated in one experience onto sticky notes, they are able to lift and drop them into another, making unexpected connections and realizing new potential.

A variety of digital tools contain and enrich our efforts to make writing as well. For instance, many writers and makers maintain blogs where they share snippets of their thinking and their work with others. They connect digitally with writers beyond our community to receive feedback and expand their learning networks.

Some students curate resources online, relying on social bookmarking tools like Diigo to organize, archive, and share links to the digital texts that inform their work. They create Livebinders for similar purposes. Pinterest and FlickR allow users to communicate visually, and we've been using them in increasingly inventive ways. Online tools also inspire all kinds of making. As dynamic and empowering as these tools are, we find that they tend to supplement rather than supplant the containers we build out of composition books, sticky notes, file folders, and paper.

WHAT YOU CAN DO TOMORROW

- **Show writers how to tinker.** Begin by helping them select just one lens through which they will examine their own writing. Perhaps they'll study idea development, organization, voice, sentence fluency, word choice, character development, or using conventions for effect. Invite writers to dip into their drafts and lift out examples of the identified element. These small bits of text can be added to a writer's notebook, a new document on their laptops, or sticky notes. Once these bits are isolated, writers strive to revise them in a variety of ways. Inspiration can be gained from the work of authors who have demonstrated real craftsmanship. It's empowering to write like those we admire. Once writers have tinkered around with their writing in this way, they can invite others to review their adaptations and provide feedback. This input will help them choose the versions they will keep.

- **Introduce writers to tinkering routines.** Routines keep messy learning productive. They also help us make our thinking, learning, and processes increasingly visible. This is how communities of writers learn from one another.

The tinkering routines below are our favorites at the WNY Young Writer's Studio. They were inspired by Dave Gray, Sunni Brown, and James Macanufo, who wrote the book, *Gamestorming*. Some writers work with them independently, while others use them to engage in collaborative thinking.

OTHER BOOKS IN THE
HACK LEARNING SERIES

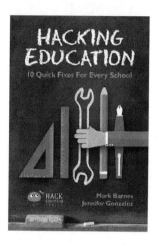

HACKING EDUCATION
10 Quick Fixes For Every School

By Mark Barnes (@markbarnes19) & Jennifer Gonzalez (@cultofpedagogy)

In the bestselling *Hacking Education*, Mark Barnes and Jennifer Gonzalez employ decades of teaching experience and hundreds of discussions with education thought leaders to show you how to find and hone the quick fixes that every school and classroom need. Using a Hacker's mentality, they provide **one Aha moment after another** with 10 Quick Fixes For Every School—solutions to everyday problems and teaching methods that any teacher or administrator can implement immediately.

"Barnes and Gonzalez don't just solve problems; they turn teachers into hackers—a transformation that is right on time."

—Don Wettrick, Author of *Pure Genius*

See
sample
Chapter 3
on
page 209

MAKE WRITING
5 Teaching Strategies That Turn Writer's Workshop Into a Maker Space

By Angela Stockman (@angelastockman)

Everyone's favorite education blogger and writing coach, Angela Stockman, turns teaching strategies and practices upside down in the bestselling, *Make Writing*. She spills you out of your chair, shreds your lined paper, and launches you and your writer's workshop into the maker space! Stockman provides five right-now writing strategies that reinvent instruction and **inspire both young and adult writers** to express ideas with tools that have rarely, if ever, been considered. *Make Writing* is a fast-paced journey inside Stockman's Western New York Young Writer's Studio, alongside the students there who learn how to write and how to make, employing Stockman's unique teaching methods.

"Offering suggestions for using new materials in old ways, thoughtful questions, and specific tips for tinkering and finding new audiences, this refreshing book is inspiring and practical in equal measure."

—Amy Ludwig VanDerwater, Author and Teacher

HACKING ASSESSMENT
10 Ways to Go Gradeless in a Traditional Grades School

By Starr Sackstein (@mssackstein)

In the bestselling *Hacking Assessment,* award-winning teacher and world-renowned formative assessment expert Starr Sackstein unravels one of education's oldest mysteries: How to assess learning without grades—even in a school that uses numbers, letters, GPAs, and report cards. While many educators can only muse about the possibility of a world without grades, teachers like Sackstein are **reimagining education**. In this unique, eagerly-anticipated book, Sackstein shows you exactly how to create a remarkable no-grades classroom like hers, a vibrant place where students grow, share, thrive, and become independent learners who never ask, "What's this worth?"

"The beauty of the book is that it is not an empty argument against grades—but rather filled with valuable alternatives that are practical and will help to refocus the classroom on what matters most."

—Adam Bellow, White House Presidential Innovation Fellow

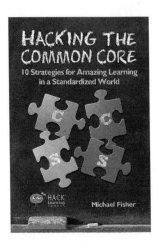

HACKING THE COMMON CORE
10 Strategies for Amazing Learning in a
Standardized World

By Michael Fisher (@fisher1000)

In *Hacking the Common Core,* longtime teacher and CCSS specialist Mike Fisher shows you how to bring fun back to learning, with 10 amazing hacks for teaching all Core subjects, while engaging students and making learning fun. Fisher's experience and insights help teachers and parents better understand close reading, balancing fiction and nonfiction, using projects with the Core, and much more. *Hacking the Common Core* provides **read-tonight-implement-tomorrow strategies** for teaching the standards in fun and engaging ways, improving teaching and learning for students, parents, and educators.

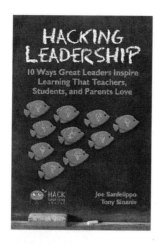

HACKING LEADERSHIP
10 Ways Great Leaders Inspire Learning That Teachers, Students, and Parents Love

By Joe Sanfelippo (@joesanfelippoFC) and Tony Sinanis (@tonysinanis)

In the runaway bestseller *Hacking Leadership*, renowned school leaders Joe Sanfelippo and Tony Sinanis bring readers inside schools that few stakeholders have ever seen—places where students not only come first but have a unique voice in teaching and learning. Sanfelippo and Sinanis ignore the bureaucracy that stifles many leaders, focusing instead on building a culture of **engagement, transparency, and most important, fun**. *Hacking Leadership* has superintendents, principals, and teacher leaders around the world employing strategies they never before believed possible.

"The authors do a beautiful job of helping leaders focus inward, instead of outward. This is an essential read for leaders who are, or want to lead, learner-centered schools."

—George Couros, Author of *The Innovator's Mindset*

HACKING LITERACY
5 Ways To Turn Any Classroom Into a Culture Of Readers

By Gerard Dawson (@gerarddawson3)

In *Hacking Literacy*, classroom teacher, author, and reading consultant Gerard Dawson reveals 5 simple ways any educator or parent can turn even the most reluctant reader into a thriving, enthusiastic lover of books. Dawson cuts through outdated pedagogy and standardization, turning reading theory into practice, sharing **valuable reading strategies**, and providing what *Hack Learning Series* readers have come to expect—actionable, do-it-tomorrow strategies that can be built into long-term solutions.

HACKING ENGAGEMENT
50 Tips & Tools to Engage Teachers and Learners Daily

By James Alan Sturtevant (@jamessturtevant)

Some students hate your class. Others are just bored. Many are too nice, or too afraid, to say anything about it. Don't let it bother you; it happens to the best of us. But now, it's **time to engage!** In *Hacking Engagement*, the seventh book in the *Hack Learning Series*, veteran high school teacher, author, and popular podcaster James Sturtevant provides 50—that's right five-oh—tips and tools that will engage even the most reluctant learners daily.

HACKING HOMEWORK
10 Strategies That Inspire Learning Outside the Classroom

By Starr Sackstein (@mssackstein) and Connie Hamilton (@conniehamilton)

Learning outside the classroom is being reimagined, and student engagement is better than ever. World-renowned author/educator Starr Sackstein has changed how teachers around the world look at traditional grades. Now she's teaming with veteran educator, curriculum director, and national presenter Connie Hamilton to bring you **10 powerful strategies** for teachers and parents that promise to inspire independent learning at home, without punishments or low grades.

"Starr Sackstein and Connie Hamilton have assembled a book full of great answers to the question, 'How can we make homework engaging and meaningful?'"

—Doug Fisher and Nancy Frey, Authors and Presenters

HACKING PROJECT BASED LEARNING
10 Easy Steps to PBL and Inquiry in the Classroom

By Ross Cooper (@rosscoops31) and Erin Murphy (@murphysmusings5)

As questions and mysteries around PBL and inquiry continue to swirl, experienced classroom teachers and school administrators Ross Cooper and Erin Murphy have written a book that will empower those intimidated by PBL to cry, "I can do this!" while at the same time providing added value for those who are already familiar with the process. *Hacking Project Based Learning* demystifies what PBL is all about with **10 hacks that construct a simple path** that educators and students can easily follow to achieve success.

"*Hacking Project Based Learning* is a classroom essential. Its ten simple 'hacks' will guide you through the process of setting up a learning environment in which students will thrive from start to finish."

—Daniel H. Pink, *New York Times* Bestselling Author of *DRIVE*

HACK LEARNING ANTHOLOGY
Innovative Solutions for Teachers and Leaders

Edited by Mark Barnes (@markbarnes19)

Anthology brings you the most innovative education Hacks from the first nine books in the *Hack Learning Series*. Written by twelve award-winning classroom teachers, principals, superintendents, college instructors, and international presenters, *Anthology* is every educator's new problem-solving handbook. It is both a preview of nine other books and a **full-fledged, feature-length blueprint** for solving your biggest school and classroom problems.

HACKING GOOGLE FOR EDUCATION
99 Ways to Leverage Google Tools in Classrooms, Schools, and Districts

By Brad Currie (@bradmcurrie), Billy Krakower (@wkrakower), and Scott Rocco (@ScottRRocco)

If you could do more with Google than search, what would it be? Would you use Google Hangouts to connect students to cultures around the world? Would you finally achieve a paperless workflow with Classroom? Would you inform and engage stakeholders district-wide through Blogger? Now, you can say Yes to all of these, because Currie, Krakower, and Rocco remove the limits in Hacking Google for Education, giving you **99 Hacks in 33 chapters**, covering Google in a unique way that benefits all stakeholders.

"Connected educators have long sought a comprehensive resource for implementing blended learning with G Suite. *Hacking Google for Education* superbly delivers with a plethora of classroom-ready solutions and linked exemplars."

—Dr. Robert R. Zywicki, Superintendent of Weehawken Township School District

HACKING ENGAGEMENT AGAIN
50 Teacher Tools That Will Make Students Love Your Class

By James Alan Sturtevant (@jamessturtevant)

50 Student Engagement Hacks just weren't enough. 33-year veteran classroom teacher, James Alan Sturtevant, wowed teachers with the original Hacking Engagement, which contained 50 Tips and Tools to Engage Teachers and Learners Daily. Those educators and students got better, but they craved more. So, longtime educator and wildly popular student engager Sturtevant is *Hacking Engagement Again*!

"This book is packed with ideas that can be implemented right away: Some creatively weave technology into instruction, others are just plain creative, and all of them are smart. Plus, the QR codes take the reader to so many more fantastic resources. With this book in hand, every teacher will find ways to freshen up their teaching and make it fun again!"

—Jennifer Gonzalez, Bestselling Author, Speaker, and CEO at CultOfPedagogy.com

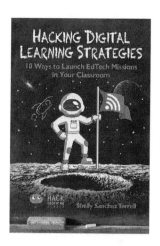

HACKING DIGITAL LEARNING STRATEGIES
10 Ways to Launch EdTech Missions in Your Classroom

By Shelly Sanchez Terrell (@ShellTerrell)

In *Hacking Digital Learning Strategies,* international EdTech presenter and NAPW Woman of the Year Shelly Sanchez Terrell demonstrates the power of EdTech Missions—lessons and projects that inspire learners to use web tools and social media to innovate, research, collaborate, problem-solve, campaign, crowd fund, crowdsource, and publish. The 10 Missions in *Hacking DLS* are more than enough to transform how teachers integrate technology, but there's also much more here. Included in the book is a **38-page Mission Toolkit,** complete with reproducible mission cards, badges, polls, and other handouts that you can copy and distribute to students immediately.

"The secret to Shelly's success as an education collaborator on a global scale is that she shares information most revered by all educators, information that is original, relevant, vetted, and proven, combining technology with proven education methodology in the classroom. This book provides relevance to a 21st century educator."

—Thomas Whitby, Author, Podcaster, Blogger, Consultant, Co-founder of #Edchat

HACKING PARENTHOOD
10 Mantras You Can Use Daily to Reduce the Stress of Parenting

By Kimberley Moran (@kimberleygmoran)

You throw out consequences willy nilly. You're tired of solutions that are all or nothing. You're frustrated with the daily chaos. Enter mantras, invaluable parenting anchors wrapped in tidy packages. These will become your go-to tools to calm your mind, focus your parenting, and concentrate on what you want for your kids. Kimberley Moran is a parent and a teacher who works tirelessly to find best practices for simplifying parenting and maximizing parent-child communication. Using **10 Parent Mantras as cues to stop time and reset**, Moran shares concrete ways to parent with intention and purpose, without losing your cool.

HACKING CLASSROOM MANAGEMENT
10 Ideas To Help You Become the Type of Teacher They Make Movies About

By Mike Roberts (@baldroberts)

Utah English Teacher of the Year and sought-after speaker Mike Roberts brings you 10 quick and easy classroom management hacks that will make your classroom the place to be for all your students. He shows you how to create an amazing learning environment that actually makes discipline, rules and consequences obsolete, no matter if you're a new teacher or a 30-year veteran teacher.

"Mike writes from experience; he's learned, sometimes the hard way, what works and what doesn't, and he shares those lessons in this fine little book. The book is loaded with specific, easy-to-apply suggestions that will help any teacher create and maintain a classroom where students treat one another with respect, and where they learn."

—Chris Crowe, English Professor at BYU, Past President of ALAN, author of Death Coming Up the Hill, Getting Away with Murder: The True Story of the Emmett Till Case; Mississippi Trial, 1955; and many other YA books

HACK LEARNING RESOURCES

All Things Hack Learning:

hacklearning.org

The Entire *Hack Learning Series* on Amazon:

hacklearningbooks.com

The Hack Learning Podcast, hosted by Mark Barnes:

hacklearningpodcast.com

Hack Learning on Twitter

@HackMyLearning

#HackLearning

#HackingLeadership

#HackingLiteracy

#HackingEngagement

#HackingHomework

#HackingPBL

#MakeWriting

#HackGoogleEdu

#EdTechMissions

#ParentMantras

#MovieTeacher

Hack Learning on Facebook:

facebook.com/hacklearningseries

Hack Learning on Instagram:

hackmylearning

The Hack Learning Academy:

hacklearningacademy.com

ABOUT THE AUTHOR

 **Angela Stockman** is a writer, teacher, and professional learning service provider. Over the last decade, she's supported teachers of writing in over seventy different school districts throughout the United States and Canada. Angela's areas of expertise include curriculum design, instructional coaching, formative assessment design, standards-based grading, and pedagogical documentation. The author of *Make Writing: 5 Strategies That Turn Writer's Workshop into a Maker Space*, Angela founded The WNY Young Writers' Studio, a community of writers and teachers of writing in western New York State.

She enjoys helping other school and community leaders design, launch, and sustain similar spaces within and beyond the four walls of their schools. Angela has taught at the graduate level, she has supervised student teachers, and she has led curriculum and assessment design initiatives inside of multiple university departments. She also works with business and nonprofit leaders to craft and share meaningful narratives about the organizations they serve. You may find Angela on Twitter, Facebook, LinkedIn, and Google+. She also blogs in her own space: www.angelastockman.com.

PUBLICATIONS

Times 10 is helping all education stakeholders improve every aspect of teaching and learning. We are committed to solving big problems with simple ideas. We bring you content from experts, shared through multiple channels, including books, podcasts, and an array of social networks. Our mantra is simple: Read it today; fix it tomorrow. Stay in touch with us at HackLearning.org, at #HackLearning on Twitter, and on the Hack Learning Facebook group.

Made in the USA
Middletown, DE
08 April 2018